WHY DO I FIND MYSELF IN THESE SITUATIONS?

Harold Alston

Lieutenant Colonel, USAF, Retired

ISBN 978-1-63844-925-6 (paperback)
ISBN 978-1-63844-926-3 (digital)

Christian Faith Publishing, Inc.
832 Park Avenue
Meadville, PA 16335
www.christianfaithpublishing.com

Printed in the United States of America

CONTENTS

★

FOREWORD

★

On a cold dark winter morning in the early 1960s, two young lieu-tenants, not long out of flight school, had just completed the pre-flight and "cocking" of their F-86Ls for runway alert shift at the Utah ANG Base. Our mission was interior defense. We were not expecting to fly since the airfield was barely above minimums. Clover control was allowed to scramble the alert birds to exercise the system but not in marginal weather. We had just called ready status to Clover when the Klaxon horn blared. We scrambled! We were IFR all the way to forty thousand feet, and we landed with ice on the radomes. The squadron commander and the operations officer both met us on the ramp and chewed us out for flying on a very bad day. We plead, "But, sir, we thought it was for real."

Harold and I started preflight training as aviation cadets, six weeks apart, at Lackland AFB, Texas, in 1957. Our ANG unit sent over twenty young men to pilot training over a two-year period. While serving together in the UANG, we had many opportunities to fly together, including holiday flybys, air shows, and mission inter-cept missions. I would fly on his wing any day, if he would have me. Harold was recalled to active duty during the Cuban crisis.

Most pilots describe flying as hours of boredom interrupted by moments of stark terror. Harold and I are among those who have "joined the tumbling mirth of sun-split clouds and done a hundred things you have not dreamed of" (quotation from "High Flight" by John G. Magee Jr.).

Harold has done all of the above and more and lived to tell us with these unique true stories.

Gary C. Nelson, Brigadier General, Retired
Assistant Adjutant General for Air
Utah National Guard

In the late 1950s, the 191st Fighter Interceptor Squadron, Utah Air National Guard, was an elite unit whose pilots scored high in annual air force gunnery competitions. It was comprised of pilots from World War II, pilots who transferred to the Air Guard from other services, Korean era pilots coming off air force active duty, and a fourth group of men who had been selected for pilot training, which they completed and then returned to ANG squadrons as second lieutenants and rated pilots. Harold Alston was one of those returning pilots. To the young aviators, the Guard was a jet country club. They attended classes at the University of Utah in the morning and then rushed to the squadron to be assigned, by the operations officer, to experienced flight leaders for training in the F-86.

Lieutenant Alston, with excellent eyesight and athletic ability, combined with a very competitive spirit quickly became proficient in the F-86 Sabre jet. During his training period, I enjoyed many flights with this enthusiastic and very competent young man. Harold went on to an illustrious career as an Air Force fighter pilot. He was the first pilot to fly one hundred combat missions over North Vietnam in the F-104, instructed fighter pilots of the German and Royal Saudi Air Forces, flew two years with a Canadian fighter squadron, and commanded the 65th Fighter Weapons Squadron (Aggressor) at Nellis Air Force Base—"the home of the fighter pilot." It has been a pleasure knowing and flying with this remarkable man.

Kendall Hopkins,
Fighter Pilot and Delta Airline Captain, Retired
St. George, Utah

As the Korean War was ending in 1953, I received my pilot wings at Laredo Air Force Base (AFB) Texas. I was sent to fighter gunnery school at Nellis AFB, Nevada. When the Korean armistice was signed, I was sent to George AFB, California. It was the fighter base with most of the experienced Korean War pilots. I was privileged to fly against several of them—for instance, Joe McConnell, the war's leading ace for shooting down sixteen MIGs, Pete Fernandez with fourteen and one half MIG victories, Bob Hoover, an ace who became a famous air show pilot, and many others.

When I left the Air Force, I transferred to the 191st Fighter Squadron, Utah Air National Guard, in Salt Lake City, Utah. They flew F-86E Sabrejets. That was the same type as were flown in Korea by the aces.

I liked to fly solo and look for "victims" that I could engage in a dogfight. As I made my attack, I always thought, *Okay, let's see what you've got.*

Toward the end of my career as a fighter pilot in the squadron, I flew with a young fighter pilot by the name of Harold R. Alston. I can say, without hesitation, that he was a pilot that had "the right stuff."

Robert Condie, Fighter Pilot,
Entrepreneur, Real Estate Developer
Salt Lake City, Utah

It has been said that great fighter pilots are born and not just trained. These kinds of fighter pilots seem to be "one" with the aircraft and seem able to unify senses of sight, touch, and mental coordination into a oneness that causes the aircraft to respond to the pilot's will. Harold Alston was one of this "rare breed."

Harold is also strongly patriotic. He knew that "freedom is not free," and he was willing to put his life on the line in defending and preserving freedom not only for the USA but also for other freedom-loving people worldwide.

I have had the privilege of knowing Harold Alston ever since Air Force flight school. We have remained friends in our post air force years. As you read this book, you will get a glimpse into the life of a great fighter pilot and a great man.

Thales A. "Tad" Derrick,
Lieutenant Colonel, USAF, Retired
Call Sign "Meteor"

ACKNOWLEDGMENTS

★

I dedicate this narrative first and foremost to my family for their never-ending support and for everything I have done, including this work. Thanks to my wife, Patsy, and our pilot sons, Doug, Brad, Russ, and Rod, for their help and encouragement. Each is very successful in his own profession and with their own family. We are a happy family! A few of our grandchildren have read my combat journal entries and have made encouraging comments for the preservation of them and the photos in my scrapbook. This book documents more of my flying history.

I also want to recognize my debt to friends, associates, church leaders, scout leaders, air force buddies, and all who have touched my life in any way. There are too many to name and some who are no longer living but are not forgotten. Many have encouraged me to write about my experiences and are anxious to see the finished copy.

I cannot praise proofreaders and other helpers enough. Without their insights and suggestions, these stories would never have been completed. They were generous with their time and encouragement. First is my wife, Patsy, who expertly proofread and offered suggestions while persevering before and during her deteriorating health. Unfortunately, she did not see the completed work. Dr. Ray Alston (grandson), a Russian language professor at Ohio State University, gave scholarly critics and suggestions. Brad Alston, who knows computers inside and out, fixed problems I created. He also selected book format, photos, and many hours in perfecting the presentation and accuracy as well as encouraging additional stories. Amy Alston, a wonderful daughter-in-law with professional skills and a university degree in communication, corrected many of my drafts and offered intelligent changes that I did not hesitate to honor. Carly Alston (granddaughter), a third-year university student, expertly helped with punctuation and sentence structure. Last but not least, Lindsay Alston (granddaughter), a summa cum laude university graduate, spent numerous weekend hours doing rewrites, reformatting, computer processes, and positive encouragement to finish the project. I could not have attempted nor finished this work without each of their generous contributions.

I am indebted to all my helpers. A thousand thanks is a large number, but in this case, I don't think it is enough.

I love each of you and wish you well in your own personal contributions and challenges.

INTRODUCTION

★

When I was young, I built model airplanes, looked at airplane pictures, and read stories about flying. I admired and envied pilots but thought it was beyond my abilities and desires to be one. Finally, quite by chance, an opportunity presented itself while I was an airman second class training as a radio repairman in the 130th Aircraft Control and Warning (AC&W) Squadron in the Utah Air National Guard (UANG). Richard Kendall, who would later be best man at my wedding, and I cut classes and went to the flight line to watch the pilots of the 191st Fighter Squadron fly their F-86E Sabrejets. The airplanes were beautiful, and the pilots were very cool wearing parachutes and carrying their jet helmets. Something changed when Richard said, "Why don't we apply for the Aviation Cadet Program and earn our pilot wings?" We did and were accepted. I was nineteen years old and had never been in an airplane.

Jet pilots

To see if I could tolerate flying, I asked a fellow airman who had just received his private pilot license if he would take me for a flight. He said yes even though he had only logged forty hours in a Cessna 140. I loved the hour that we flew, did not get airsick, and decided if he could fly an airplane, so could I. Before departing for training, I also got a flight in a T-33 jet trainer with the fighter squadron commander. The airline flight from Salt Lake City, Utah, to San Antonio, Texas, to become a cadet was my third flight in an airplane. Did I really make the right choice? It remained to be seen.

I was awarded my silver air force pilot wings and gold bars of a second lieutenant on August 29, 1957. I was now a commissioned officer and a fully rated jet pilot.

I began my training in 1956 and retired from the air force on January 1, 1982. I flew my last civilian flight on April 22, 2011. That was fifty-five years of flying, not bad for a teenager who did not think he could pass the initial qualifying examinations.

The following short narratives are all true. I have not enhanced any of them to make them sound more dangerous, more difficult, or more impressive. They are just some of my favorite flying memories. As part of my personal history, I record them for my own pleasure. However, if you enjoy reading them, I will be a happy clam.

CHAPTER 1

★

Mariana, Florida

FIRST SOLO

After three months of preflight military training at Lackland Air Force Base (AFB) in San Antonio, Texas, I was transferred to Graham Air Base (AB) in Mariana, Florida. The first airplane in which I trained was the Beech T-34 Mentor. It had a low wing with a 225-horsepower piston-driven engine, retractable landing gear, flaps, and controls in the front and back cockpits. Unlike the three other flights I experienced, my first flight was all mine. I made the takeoff, flew the air work, and made the landings. Even flying at 140 knots (161 mph) and only 80 knots (92 mph) on final approach, I was really busy. It was all new to me, and there was a lot to think about every second. Thankfully, the instructor was constantly telling me what to do and how to do it.

Beech T-34 Mentor

I guess because my last name started with *A*, I was usually assigned the first flight of the day. After a total of seven hours, my instructor told me to taxi to the ramp but not to park the airplane. He instructed me to go solo, stay in the traffic pattern, and make three landings while he watched from the ground. I was not nervous (ha ha), but I certainly was alert trying to remember everything I had been taught in the previous seven hours of flying.

The first takeoff and landing went well. I retracted the landing gear and continued to climb eight hundred feet to downwind. The airplane felt a little sluggish compared to the previous takeoff. I was busy with radio calls, checking engine instruments, and airspeed indicator to see why I had that feeling. Everything looked fine, so I continued the pattern. I extended the landing gear on downwind opposite my landing spot. Everything was normal with three green lights indicating the landing gear was down and locked. My airspeed was good, but it required a little more power than I remembered on the first landing.

After lining up with the runway on my final approach, I reached for the flap lever, but the flaps were already down. Yikes, what a dummy. I had forgotten to retract the flaps after the first landing. I was not smart enough with my minimum experience to figure it out. I should have formed a procedural pattern when safely airborne to retract the landing gear, check that they were up, check the airspeed, and then retract the flaps. In that small airplane when the flaps retracted, the airplane lost lift. To compensate, I pulled up the nose slightly, and because of the additional drag, acceleration was diminished. With my limited experience, I knew zilch about lift and drag but was beginning to learn little by little.

My third pattern and landing went well, I remembered to retract the flaps before getting airborne, and the airplane reacted just the way it should. I never forgot the flaps again. Even with the instructor watching from the ground, he did not notice my mistake and congratulated me on being the first cadet to go solo. I never did tell my instructor about the flap problem. I earned the traditional reward: my classmates threw me into the swimming pool fully dressed in flying suit and boots. What a way to celebrate my first solo flight. However, it only happens once in a lifetime.

I considered myself a pilot, albeit still a student pilot, and completed my training in the T-34 with the designated syllabus time of forty hours. I logged eighteen hours dual, twenty-two hours solo, and ninety-one landings.

COCKPIT SMOKE—LOST

The second phase of primary pilot training was also at Graham AB in Florida, but it was in a more advanced airplane. The North American T-28 Trojan had a two-seat tandem cockpit and a big (at least to me) radial engine with 750 horsepower. It was larger than the T-34, and we had to use the built-in steps to climb into the cockpit. It was noisier, had a fair amount of torque when applying power, and had a much faster and more exciting spin. The more aggressively you applied rudder and stick to break the spin, the faster it recovered.

North American T-28 Trojan

It felt like I was sitting in a World War II fighter, and it flew like one. It was faster, more fun to do acrobatics, had more visibility, and was more fun to land. This phase required one hundred hours. I made 142 landings, flew 53.4 hours dual, 46.5 hours solo, 25 hours of instrument time, and 8 hours at night.

It was in this airplane that I experienced my first abnormal situation. The first came early in my dual checkout with my instructor, Mr. "Flaps" Laffert, a civilian contract instructor. I learned a lot from him, but we were quite opposite in our demeanors and personalities. (He was short on patience, a big party animal, and a former navy pilot.) Swear words were everyday language for him. He was my instructor, not my friend. I was happier when I flew solo.

Solo in a T-28

It was a typical day flight to practice aircraft control, acrobatics, and a few practice landings. Before we started the air work, the cockpit filled with a light smoke and heavy odor of something electrical. In this instance, Flaps did not yell or even talk over the intercom but passed me a note to turn off all electrical equipment, slide the canopy open, and return to the airport. I was finished with that flight when he took control, flew back to Graham AB, and made a safe landing with no radio and no electrically operated systems.

Later in the course, our training included solo navigation flights outside of the practice area, departing and returning to Graham AB. The established routes were over northern Florida and southern Georgia. My first cross-country flight went exactly as planned. I found each turning point, and my elapsed times between checkpoints were accurate.

The next day, I flew the same route, only the opposite direction. All went well until I got over the southern part of Georgia. I looked at the ground and recognized some rocky cliffs that I had seen the day before. Since they were on my left during the first flight, I thought I must have drifted off course on the second flight. So I corrected to the north, putting the cliffs on my right. At the time that I should have been over the next turning point, it was not there. I got a shot of adrenalin because I was not where I should have been. Was I lost?

I started to circle, looked for my turn point, and spotted a town north of my position just two or three miles away. We had a procedure that if we got lost, we called the airborne instructors for help. I did so, and before they had come very far toward me, I identified from my map the town as Americus, Georgia. It was not very far north of my proposed turning point, so I turned back south to find my proper course for the last leg. Knowing where I was, I no longer needed the instructors. They made sure I knew my exact location and called off their search rendezvous.

The rest of the flight was without incident. At dinner that evening, my "lost" incident was brought up in front of all the cadets in the dining hall. This was routine exposure to the daily bloopers. It was embarrassing, but I rationalized my remarks by saying I was not lost but momentarily disoriented. It brought a lot of jeers from my classmates.

The takeaway for me was that there are a lot of places that look the same from either direction, rely on your skills, and have confidence in your navigation. I never should have thought I was off course or used the ground in that area for reference. The last thing was for me to admit I made a mistake and not rationalize my way out of it. Fortunately, it was a valuable lesson learned and never happened again.

CHAPTER 2

★

Greenville, Mississippi

FINALLY... JETS!

The final phase of pilot training was at Greenville, Mississippi. The base had been closed for years and was reactivated. I was in the second class of cadets after the reopening. We had an upper class to harass us but no lower class for us to harass. At least we were now in jet trainers and were treated much better than the hazing we experienced in the preflight phase. Greenville was on the mighty Mississippi River, so it was impossible to get lost. As cadets, we could come and go as we wished when we were off duty. We could enjoy the services of town, boating on Lake Ferguson, formed by the river, and our instructors were military pilots instead of civilians. I even bought a 1955 Oldsmobile there, so I had my own transportation.

This assignment was also a reunion of Utah cadets. We were all together in preflight. Craig Iverson and I did our primary training at Graham AB, Mariana, Florida, but Tad Derrick was trained at Malden, Missouri. Craig and I were roommates, and Tad and I were on group staff together as the ranking leaders of our class. We remain good friends today.

Utah Cadets: Alston, Derrick, and Iverson

I was excited to begin this final phase of training because it was in a jet. I had looked forward to flying jets for a long time, and this was my first chance. The T-33, commonly called the T-Bird, had a single engine, two seats in tandem, a clamshell canopy, 120 knot (138 mph) final approach speed, top speed of .8 Mach (8/10 the speed of sound), capable to climb to 40,000 feet, and was fully acrobatic. We flew with jet helmets equipped with a sun visor, oxygen mask, and built-in microphone, and earphones. We buckled on a parachute and sat on an ejection seat.

Front seat flying the T-33

I was trained by two different instructors. Pat Harrison was a second lieutenant who received his wings one year ahead of me. Abner Proffit was my other instructor with about the same experience. We became good friends and even went water skiing on Lake Ferguson with Pat and his motorboat. Academics included learning all about airplane systems, capabilities, limitations, procedures, meteorology, and navigation. When academics were completed with final exams, our time was spent on the flight line or in physical training. The more squares filled, the easier the training became and more casual time we were able to enjoy.

My training went very well, and when I flew my first solo, after minimum syllabus flights, I was in hog heaven. I had completed one of my five goals that I made when I was a teenager which was to fly a jet airplane, one time, all by myself. I did it. There were many more to come, which added icing to the cake.

Transition was easy; formation was easier. My instructor cleared me to fly solo formation after two dual training flights instead of four that the syllabus required. Instrument flying was no problem because of several hours of instrument practice in the Link Trainers. Acrobatics were a blast, and I really enjoyed doing loops and rolls. Except for instrument training flights, I think I performed a roll or went upside down on almost every flight.

I enjoyed flying with Pat. He was an aggressive instructor, and more than once, we buzzed Walnut, Mississippi, his hometown. Spins in a jet were never part of any training program. Pat thought I should see what it was like and learn how to recover from one if it happened inadvertently. We never talked about it on the ground, so I do not know if I was the only student in my class to spin the T-33. It was a fun and daring experience and would not be the last time I had to recover from a spin.

Abner Proffit also was a good instructor who demanded excellence and did not tolerate sloppy flying. We were practicing lazy eights one day, which is a vertical maneuver. The first part of the maneuver requires a constant climb, increasing bank, and constant change of airspeed with the nose coming through the horizon in a ninety-degree bank. The other half of the horizontal eight was just the opposite. It is difficult to do perfectly.

Abner was not satisfied with my performance and had me level out. He said, "Mr. Alston, what do you see down by your feet?" Confused by the question, I finally said, "Rudder pedals." His response in a very loud voice was, "*Then use the*—!" Until that experience, I never had to use much rudder in the jet because there was very little torque.

A maneuver like the lazy eight requires the rudder to maintain coordination to avoid slips and skids. He had me sing "(Up a) Lazy River" while performing the maneuver. It really helped, and I became very good at lazy eights. I never forgot how to fly the maneuver with what I learned from Abner, and I used his suggestions in other airplanes in which I instructed. It really paid off when I checked out in the F-5E at Williams AFB in 1976. The flight examiner had me fly a lazy eight on my final check flight. I sang the song Abner taught me to use and was graded "a perfect lazy eight." The examiner said it was the first time he had seen that maneuver flown perfectly. Thanks, Abner!

Having passed all phases of training, the last hurdle was an air force instrument check flight. Passing that important flight placed us in the "No Sweat Club" assuring us of graduating as air force pilots certified to fly in clouds and bad weather. My final evaluation was a two-hour flight under a hood, so I could not see out of the airplane, concluding with a low frequency radio approach to landing. I thought I did a good job, but the flight examiner did not say anything as we walked to the squadron. Finally, I could stand it no longer and could not wait for the debriefing to find out if I had passed. I turned to him and asked, "Sir, did I pass?" He looked at me, smiled, and said only one word: "Yes." I was so relieved.

My T-33 flying time totaled 105 hours which included 34 hours of instrument flying, 6 hours at night, and 79 landings. At that time, the entire pilot training course took 18 months at three different locations with 245 total flying hours in three different airplanes.

Graduation was on August 29, 1957. Mother, Dad, my sister, Celia, and my fiancée, Patsy, came by train to Greenville for the event. Mother and Dad pinned on my gold second lieutenant bars, and Patsy pinned on my pilot wings. I was twenty-one years and eight months of age and got married eighteen days later.

Mom pinning the bars!

Patsy pins the wings!

CHAPTER 3

★

Sherman, Texas

FIRST FLIGHT EMERGENCY

Since I went to pilot training from the Air National Guard (ANG), my assignment was based on returning to the Utah 191st Fighter Squadron. They had been flying the F-86E model which was a day fighter but were scheduled to convert to the F-86L and become an all-weather fighter interceptor squadron. That resulted in my being sent to Perrin AFB, Sherman, Texas, to become qualified in the airplane and the new mission.

North American F-86L Sabre

The training at Perrin was in two phases. Initially, we received about thirty hours of solid instrument flying because as an all-weather interceptor pilot, we could be expected to scramble at a moment's notice and fly in all kinds of weather.

The main training started with several hours in a cockpit simulator exactly like the real F-86L. With the canopy closed, we were totally on instruments. I learned the cockpit layout of switches, levers, instruments, etc., and flew it like we would fly the actual airplane including the radar.

After all the training leading up to flying the real airplane, my day finally arrived. I was ready for my first flight and was about to realize my long-awaited dream of flying a jet fighter all by myself. I was not nervous but eager to get on with it.

I walked to my assigned aircraft with my instructor. We noticed that I had been assigned the wing commander's personal aircraft. There is nothing like having the best-looking and probably the best maintained airplane in the fleet. My instructor shadowed me on the preflight inspection to make sure I did not miss anything. I climbed in the cockpit and strapped in. My instructor reviewed the cockpit check before going to his airplane. Engine start was normal. I got taxi instructions, and my instructor followed behind me to the end of the runway. The tower cleared us for takeoff, and away we went.

I released brakes and accelerated down the runway with my instructor ten seconds behind me. Everything was normal breaking ground. Gear and flaps up, climb speed attained, I came out of afterburner and saw my instructor in chase position.

I headed for the training area, maintaining a good lookout for other airplanes and nailing the climb speed. It seemed easier than the simulator and a heck of a lot more fun. Entering the practice area, our planned altitude was twenty-five thousand feet. There was not a cloud in the sky.

As I passed through twenty thousand feet with everything quite normal, I was surprised when the fire warning light on the top of the instrument panel illuminated bright red. My first thought was that a fire was going to ruin a perfectly fun flight. However, after having practiced every possible emergency in the simulator, I reacted appropriately, reduced the throttle, and reported the problem to my instructor. He visually checked me over and did not find any sign of a fire and told me to head back to the base as a precaution.

I made my first real landing in the F-86L and taxied back to parking without incident. Emergency over and I thought "it had to be easy going the rest of the training." It turned out to be so, and every flight from then on was without complications. Who else but me has a potentially serious emergency on the first flight even though it turned out to only be a faulty warning light circuit? *Why do I find myself in these situations?*

CHAPTER 4

★

Salt Lake City, Utah

FORMATION SPIN

If you are thinking there is no such thing as a formation spin, you would be right. We fly a lot of formation in various positions including close, combat, chase, and every other conceivable position you can think of but never in a spin. This is a true story, just like every other story in this book, which led to the title of this book… *Why Do I Find Myself in These Situations?*

When I finished advanced training at Perrin AFB in the F-86L, I returned to the 191st Fighter Squadron with the UANG in Salt Lake City, Utah. The squadron was still flying the F-86E and did not receive the new L models for several months. That was great because it gave me the opportunity to fly a different fighter in the meantime.

There were a lot of differences in the two airplanes. The engines were different. The wings were different because the E had slats on the leading edge. The L was heavier and had an afterburner. The E had six 20 mm machine guns where the L had rockets. The E had a gun sight with small radar for tracking in close range. The L had no gun sight but had search radar with lock-on capability and a steering dot to fly a lethal lead collision course to fire the rockets. The E had a sliding bubble canopy; the L had a clamshell bubble canopy. The L even had a drag chute for additional deceleration on landing. But other than those differences, they flew the same. By pulling the control stack back, the airplane climbed; pushing it forward made it dive. Pushing stick to the left, it turned the airplane left and vice versa to the right. Thank goodness, that is the way all airplanes work!

North American F-86E Sabre two-ship formation

After a very quick checkout of a couple of flights, I was scheduled to fly with Kendall "Hoppy" Hopkins (an ex-navy fighter pilot and who was an airline pilot at the time of this flight) leading the flight. My contemporary, Craig Iverson, was on Hoppy's wing as number 2. Craig and I graduated from pilot training together. We were both the least experienced pilots in the squadron. Number 3 was Gary Garner—a very experienced F-86 pilot and a great air-to-air gunnery pilot. I flew number 4 on Gary's wing.

The mission was two versus two simulated aerial combat…my first ever. We had no formal briefing, so as we were going to get parachutes and helmets, I asked Gary what we were going to do. Gary was always a man of few words, so the following is almost a direct quote. He said, "We will get our slats out so we can turn better, fly toward the other two airplanes, and start the fight." That was all I needed because in an air fight, it is so fluid you cannot predict what happens after the initial engagement.

The formation takeoff and climb to twenty-five thousand feet was normal. It was a beautiful clear day, and visibility was endless.

At level-off, the two elements each turned ninety degrees in opposite directions to get spacing before turning back to engage. I was still flying close formation on Gary's left wing in a right climbing turn to reduce speed so the slats could extend as we reduced airspeed. The slats were supposed to be fully extended at 220 knots. I was still flying in close formation, and my slats were both out when suddenly Gary's nose dropped, and we were in a descending turn to the right. I thought this was crazy until Gary pulled out and left me. I looked down at the ground and immediately recognized that I was in a spin, and Gary had recovered quickly while I went around two more turns before I recovered from the spin, got the nose back level, and accelerated for more airspeed. I could not believe that I had still been flying close formation while we were spinning. It was the first and the last time I ever spun an F-86 Sabre jet.

I spotted the other aircraft and headed to rejoin my leader while Craig was below and out of the fight. Hoppy and Gary were in hard turns pulling several Gs (forces of gravity) and maneuvering hard to get on each other's tail. I did not know who was who, and by the time I got back in their area, the fight was over. I still do not know who won, but it looked like a stalemate. I rejoined on Gary's wing; Craig found us and joined on Hoppy, and we headed home. I certainly did not learn much about air fighting, but I learned to move into combat formation sooner and not fly close formation going into a fight.

Postscript: At the next squadron meeting with the commander, operations (Ops) officer, flight commanders, and all the pilots, Hopkins raised his hand and said he wanted to make a statement. He stood and talked about my flying close formation in a spin—something he had never seen before and never would see again. However, he chastised me for not recovering from the spin sooner and getting in the fight with my leader. Everyone got a good laugh and was amazed that I had spun the Sabrejet for two turns, in formation, before recovering. My advice is to never try it yourself.

THE GOOD OLD DAYS

Throughout my life, I have always heard people, regardless of their profession, reflect on the "good old days." Curiosity has caused me to try to figure out when those days were. Were they a generation ago, last century, or during one's childhood? I really don't have a satisfying answer, but perhaps, the following experience will illustrate what I mean.

Before being recalled to active duty for the Cuban Missile Crisis in 1962, I was a pilot in the 191st Fighter Interceptor Squadron, Utah Air National Guard. Our squadron flew F-86L Sabre jets as the primary mission aircraft. In addition, we possessed three T-33s for instrument practice and for support pilots to fly. I was fortunate to maintain currency in both aircraft, which was not available to every pilot in our squadron, including my flight commander.

As a young lieutenant, I really liked and respected my flight commander, Jay "Gordo" VanDam. Gordo was one generation of airplanes ahead of me because he had flown the P-51 Mustang before getting into jets and the F-86. The Sabre was my first fighter.

During a regular weekend drill period, neither Gordo nor I were scheduled to fly the F-86 but were paired together in a T-33 for a proficiency flight. I was in the front seat, and he was in the back. It was a perfect afternoon with billowy white scattered cumulus clouds over the Great Salt Lake. With the abundant heat of the day, the tops were "boiling" to about twenty thousand feet. During our flight, we eventually began to play around the clouds doing the usual things like inverted flight over the domed tops of the buildups, flying through the cloud canyons, and generally wringing off the T-Bird's tail.

Cumulus clouds

On one particular pass, I dived the aircraft for speed and pulled it into a vertical climb right up the face of a beautiful towering cloud. As we climbed, Gordo told me of the good old days when he used to do the same thing in a Mustang: not being able to outclimb the generating cloud, running out of airspeed, and entering a spin down through the cloud. I thought to myself, *I would never have a better opportunity to put a squelch on those stories.* As we neared the top of the cloud at about eighteen thousand feet, losing airspeed, I pushed on a rudder and guess what? You got it, we went into a spin, and I said casually to Gordo, "You mean like this?"

The intercom was very quiet while we spun a couple of turns in the middle of the big cloud. Then a booming voice from the cockpit behind me yelled: "Damn you, Harold, we are in a spin! Get us out of this!" I executed the normal spin recovery, on instruments, broke the rotation, and started a dive recovery. We "spit" out the side of the cloud into the clear blue sky, right over the lake, at a safe altitude. Gordo had survived his first spin in a jet aircraft and was not the least bit happy about it being in instrument meteorological conditions.

Once we were stabilized in level flight, Gordo told me, in a significantly more normal voice, "Never do that to me again." It was the only comment he ever made to me about the experience. Incidentally, he never again talked to me about the good old days either.

Postscript: Flown in 1961, written in 1992, published in 1998 in *Daedalias Flyer*—the Order of Daedalian magazine

CONDENSATION TRAIL CORKSCREW

If you have ever looked up and seen white trails being produced by jet airplanes at high altitude, you have witnessed engine exhaust being condensed in cold temperatures. They are very common but depend on the right conditions. Condensation (con) levels change and are lower in winter and higher in summer. Depending on conditions, con trails can be very dense, and at other times, you only see faint or wispy traces of white.

Contrail

Flying from the Salt Lake City Airport in an F-86L Sabre jet one evening at dusk, I spotted a very dense and persistent con trail southeast of the valley heading my way. It inspired me to make my own trail in the sky. I found the right level at about thirty-five thousand feet and identified the aircraft I was watching as an Air Force B-52 Stratofortress. No wonder it made such a distinctive trail because that aircraft has eight jet engines.

The B-52 was heading straight for Salt Lake. At that time, there was a bomb plotting site just north of the airport that was used to electronically score simulated bomb drops. We had been briefed in the squadron that we were restricted from making simulated attacks

33

on bombers inbound to the bomb plot. However, if they were out-bound, they were fair game.

I had a better plan than to make a pass on the big bomber but to enhance his trail. That way it did not matter where I got involved with it, inbound or outbound. As he came over the city, I flew a little behind him and started flying barrel rolls around his con trail while making my own trail. What was better is that the sun was low in the sky, so it looked like a giant spotlight was shining on us.

After six or eight rolls, I wanted to see my artwork. I lost altitude and was out of the con level where I could observe the display above me. The sight was fantastic, and the condensation trails from both airplanes stayed for a long time over the city.

I have often wondered how many people on the ground enjoyed the display of two bright con trails over a high-density population in the shape of a corkscrew. I will never know, but it sure was fun to paint the picture for them.

INTENTIONAL FLAMEOUT

Flameout is an aviation word for an engine shutting down. It is a serious situation depending on when it occurs. Possible causes could be fuel starvation to the engine. Compressor stalls could blow out the flame, and inadequate airflow to the engine could be a cause. It is not a trifle experience to completely lose the power that propels an airplane that weighs several thousand pounds. A flameout on takeoff at the wrong time could be catastrophic. Flameout at altitude presents the pilot time to try a restart, glide to an emergency landing, or eject and parachute down as a last resort.

For a single-engine jet, there is no training syllabus that requires shutting down the one and only engine and practicing a restart; mul-tiengine airplane training does practice shutting down an engine to fly on whatever is left and then initiate restart procedures. So, generally, a flameout is something that you hope you never experience.

Flying jets require memorizing emergency procedures. The most critical procedures are ones that require immediate action. Hesitation or having to get out a checklist could be disastrous. We memorize the "bold face" procedures: that is the whole list of the critical procedures. We were usually tested weekly so that we did not forget them. The answers must be perfect responses. No error in writing or reciting bold face procedures is tolerated. Many of them we may never have to use, if one is lucky, but we must be prepared.

I had never experienced a flameout and was very curious to use the air start procedure. I had it memorized and could go through the required steps in just a few seconds. I decided that on one of my future flights, in the F-86L Sabre, I would close the throttle and intentionally cause the engine to flameout. Stupid…maybe, because why tempt fate in case it did not start?

North American F-86L

My next opportunity was with my good friend Alan Harris as my wingman. In my briefing, I told him I was going to shut down and restart the engine just for the experience. He looked at me like I was "nuts." I gave him no argument there.

We flew the mission as planned. On the way back, I stayed at an altitude and location where I thought if the engine did not start, I would be able to glide to a dead stick landing at Hill AFB. Hill had a longer runway than the Salt Lake City airport.

Al was in close formation when I announced that I was going to shut down the engine. I closed the throttle, and the engine wound down and became very quiet. I reduced airspeed to 180 knots, which was the emergency glide speed. The silence was quite nice for a change. I clicked the radio and told Al I would attempt the restart and that I would lose the radio during that procedure. He stayed on my wing. I learned what it was like to glide in a jet fighter but was ready to return to powered flight. I activated the air start switch and advanced the throttle to get the fuel flowing. The engine started normally; I advanced the throttle and accelerated normally. With the "fun" over, we returned to Salt Lake and landed.

Alan asked a few questions about the flameout and the restart but said he would wait until it happened for real before he would attempt what I had done. Other than my wingman, Alan, I never told anyone about my intentional flameout.

It was a good learning experience, albeit not an approved one but something that gave me more confidence in my F-86L. It came in handy later in my flying career, but those are other stories.

IMITATING A TRAIN

Upon reading the title of this story, I know you are thinking that an airplane cannot, in any way, imitate a train on a railroad. Well, you are correct. Airplanes go faster, are more attractive, and are not restricted in the course and direction they must go. But…read on, my friends.

This flight occurred while I was flying with the 191st Fighter Interceptor Squadron, UANG, Salt Lake City, Utah. The airplane was an F-86L Sabre. Since it was an interceptor, part of the mission was to intercept unidentified aircraft. We were expected to perform the mission day or night and in all kinds of weather. To accomplish identification at night, the airplane was equipped with an identification light mounted in the nose. It was always retracted into the bottom of the aircraft when not in use. It was as bright as a landing light and only required a flip of a switch to extend and retract the light. It was seldom used.

I scheduled an airplane for a night flight. Night, as well as instruments, landings, etc. are part of maintaining air force currency. No one else was flying that night, so I was free to do anything I wanted. To kill time, I flew to Hill AFB for a practice instrument approach.

Being satisfied with that, I turned west and flew over the Great Salt Lake. It was very dark because there were no lights on the lake.

The lake is divided by a railroad causeway that had been constructed above the level of the water for railroad tracks. The causeway saved many miles and precious time for a direct route to the west into Nevada. The alternative would have been to lay track all the way around the northern portion of the lake increasing both time, distance, and cost to get to the same place to the other side. Geographically, it is a very large lake.

Looking at the wonder of the causeway, I saw a westbound train approaching the center of the lake. My "idea light" turned on. I wondered if the identification light on my airplane would look like a train engine light. It was probably as bright and maybe about the same size. Since there was only a single track and there was already a train on it westbound, what would the engineer think if he saw another light coming toward him?

I flew my Sabre a few miles west and lined up on the tracks heading for the westbound train. I also turned off my blinking navigation lights on the wings and tail and extended the identification light in the nose. Since the sky was clear, there was some moonlight that reflected off the steel tracks so I could see them. With a little night vision, I was comfortable flying quite low, just above the tracks, heading for the train.

I flew toward the headlight of the oncoming engine. When I got as close as I dared, I pulled up at the last second to avoid collision, turned off the identification light, turned on the navigation lights, and headed for home.

Looking back, that was a stupid thing to do. If I had misjudged, it would have been disastrous. But, on the other hand, what did the engineer driving the train think? He certainly did not hit an oncoming train. Did he think that he was just seeing things? Was he scared? Did he apply the brakes? Was it just a weird figment of his imagination? Did he see that it was an airplane buzzing him?

No complaint call was made to the squadron, so I never got in trouble. Also, I never told anyone until years later, after I retired, and then only in passing to a very good friend of mine as we hunted deer together. I will never know, but I still wonder to this day what the engineer thought seeing the "phantom train" on his track.

NIGHT FLAMEOUT

The following flight was also at night. Don Pihl and I were scheduled for a night intercept mission in F-86Ls. One of us was to act as target while the other pilot flew the intercepts. Halfway through the mission, we would reverse roles; that way, we could both practice intercepting the target. We were assigned our airplanes, and Don walked to the flight line a few minutes before me. As I approached my assigned airplane, Don was already making his preflight inspection, but it was on the airplane to which I was assigned. No problem! I told him I would take the other airplane since the crew chief was waiting for a pilot, and Don already had his parachute and helmet in the cockpit. We called operations on the radio to notify them of the change.

Takeoff and climb to altitude were normal, and we began our intercepts with ground-controlled radar giving us vectors. As we flew north in our intercepts, all was going quite well. We were over the Burley Mountains in southern Idaho when it was my turn to be the attacker.

The ground radar site vectored me for my first intercept. Looking at my radar, I found my target. Just before I locked on with radar, Don called on the radio and reported that his engine had flamed out. Yikes! He had lost engine power, and it was pitch black except for a few scattered lights on the ground and stars above us. What was worse, we were miles from Hill AFB which was the best choice for an emergency landing.

Since I had Don on my radar, I knew exactly where he was, but I had to find him visually in the dark. I told him to head for Hill AFB. As I got closer, I saw his navigation lights and joined on his wing. He established the recommended glide speed of 180 knots to get maximum range from the altitude we had. Fortunately, our intercepts had been above thirty thousand, so that was a benefit. I was confidant we could make it to Hill AFB.

Once stabilized in the glide and heading for Hill, he was ready to try an air start. I asked if he wanted me to read the checklist to him, but he assured me he knew the emergency procedure. I reminded him when he activated the air start switch he would lose the radio and voice communications between us.

The air start procedure worked as it was designed, and Don restored engine power, and the emergency was over. We decided that there was no use tempting fate, so we returned to Salt Lake. Don landed first as a precaution before anything else could go wrong. After chasing him safely to his landing, I made a go around, closed pattern, and landed behind Don.

Looking back, I recalled that Don had taken the airplane to which I was initially assigned. At the time, it seemed like no big deal because the airplanes were identical. If I had been flying it, I guess I would have had the emergency. Certainly, it was a twist of fate for a simple change in airplanes. Was Don meant to experience the emergency? Was I supposed to assume the role of escorting him to a safe landing? "Why" questions like those do not have clear answers, but at least, everything worked out well for two grateful interceptor pilots.

ARIZONA VERTIGO

When asked why we had to go on cross-country flights, the answer was always the same. It was not just on a whim to see new places, see old friends, wasting jet fuel, wasting taxpayer money, or a short weekend vacation. It was for "navigation proficiency." After all, you never know when one might be required to deploy away from home base to a strange location. You get the idea…we must be adaptable. Wives, however, sometimes did not believe the tactical reasons we gave, especially if they had other plans for us in the back of their minds. Most wives also did not place a lot of faith on the return times we told them. My wife automatically added two hours to my estimate and was usually closer to my actual return than I was. Sometimes, it was just hard to make the airplane land, if you know what I mean.

Don Jansen and I planned a cross-country flight from our home base at Salt Lake City to Williams AFB southeast of Phoenix, Arizona. Williams was a fighter base, with F-86Fs, at that time. The distance from Salt Lake was about right for the range of the F-86L, and "Willy" usually had great weather. It was a great place to visit. Unfortunately, the air force closed the base in 1993 and turned it over to the local government who made it a civil airport.

We planned to return to Salt Lake after dark so we could log time toward night currency requirements. The planned time was about one hour and twenty minutes. The preflight inspection, engine start, and taxi to the end of the runway were normal. Everything, including all the cockpit and external navigation lights, operated as designed. Don was leading the return flight.

I was quite comfortable flying night formation including close formation takeoff on the wing. However, Don told me to take off ten seconds after he rolled. We called this a snake takeoff. It was designed to see the other airplane on radar and not fly close formation which required more concentration. I was not particularly happy with this but accepted it without argument.

Takeoff was normal, and after I was airborne with the landing gear and flaps retracted, I spotted Don on radar and saw his flashing navigation lights about eight miles ahead of me. I probably should have locked on with my radar, but I really did not want to fly all the way to Salt Lake in snake formation. I wanted to get closer to Don's aircraft and just fly in spread formation where I could keep him in sight.

Between looking for Don's airplane, checking the radar, cross-checking my engine instruments, seeing the stars above and the lights scattered on the Arizona desert floor, I realized I did not know which way was up or down. The scattered lights on the desert looked just like stars. I suddenly realized I had a bad case of vertigo. Vertigo is caused by moving one's head causing the fluid in the middle ear to move and the cilia (ear hairs) to "bend' in a certain direction. It is not uncommon and is just one of the potential dangers of flying at night, in clouds, or in really bad weather when you have no discernable references.

I received vertigo training as a cadet and became familiar with the symptoms, results, and corrective procedure. Other than training in the spinning rotating chair, this was the first time I had experienced the problem. There are many accidents, even deaths, attributed to vertigo. It is not uncommon at night or in weather where one has no outside references. Even though I was in clear weather, I could not distinguish stars from the lights on the ground. I know that seems crazy, but it is true and not uncommon.

As soon as I realized I had vertigo, I did what I was trained to do…forget the outside and strictly flew on instruments. I made sure I was level, on the correct altitude, and not rolling or diving toward the ground. After a few short minutes, my inner ears settled down, and I was totally reoriented, comfortable, and breathing easy again.

I called Don and reported that I had lost him on radar and did not know where he was. With a few directions, from Don, I found him visually and moved to a closer position. I flew the rest of the way home in normal formation. I avoided looking at the stars, the ground, the radar, and checked my instruments without moving my head. I chalked up the flight to a good learning opportunity, and it never happened again in my entire career…thank goodness.

WEATHER GUINEA PIG

A guinea pig is described in the literature as having a docile nature, is friendly and responsive, and is relatively easy to care for. Therefore, it is a popular household pet. I don't look like a guinea pig, but I think I have some of the same personality characteristics especially in regard to flying. I will fly any time, with anyone, and for any reason.

Guinea pig

In the Air National Guard, the squadron and all the support members were required to attend two all-day training periods on the first Saturday and Sunday of every month. As pilots, we had some ground training, but our main effort was to fly. We always flew our F-86Ls on those weekends. On this particular day, the weather was totally overcast. That did not bother us because we were all-weather fighter interceptor pilots.

I checked the flying schedule and noticed that I was not on it. Disappointed, I wondered what I was going to do all day. While most of the other pilots were changing from their uniforms into flying suits and boots, I aimlessly roamed around the operations building until I was approached by the squadron commander. Lieutenant Colonel George Caldwell said that the weather was marginal for flying and asked if I would fly and check the weather to help decide to fly or cancel the flights. Being cooperative, friendly, and responsive, I readily accepted. Just like a guinea pig, right?

I performed the airplane preflight inspection, taxied to the runway, and took off into the clouds. I was on instruments within a thousand feet off the ground. No problem, I planned to climb to thirty-five thousand feet and see if it would be clear enough for scheduled training flights. I changed radio frequency to our radar control facility and was immediately advised that the flying schedule had been cancelled. Wow, they did not even wait for my observations and report. I guessed they had a new forecast that was worse than previously reported, but I would have suggested the same decision. The weather was lousy and would have been a wasted effort.

I was asked for my intentions since I was already airborne. Many thoughts ran through my mind. I could stay up for an hour and log more instrument flying time, but if I did and the airport weather went below minimum ceiling and visibility, I would have to divert to an alternate. The problem was usually if Salt Lake was closed, Wendover Airport and Hill AFB would also be closed. That left Nellis AFB in Las Vegas as the closest alternate. I could make it but would have been stuck there until weather improved in Salt Lake, and that was not going to happen very soon.

My solution was to fly to the approach fix and return to Salt Lake. That is what I did even though I had only been airborne for a short time. Starting my weather penetration and approach from twenty thousand feet and thirty miles south of the airport, my impression was to get on the ground as soon as possible. The descent positioned me low enough to intercept the course and glide slope of the Salt Lake instrument landing system. I still had not seen anything but clouds. As I continued the approach, I could not see the ground until I was about a half mile from the runway and only a couple of hundred feet above the ground. It was a good sight.

I landed safely and noticed, as I taxied back to the ramp to park the airplane, that it was snowing. I was happy to park the jet and return to the operations building. All is well that ends well. It was a wasted a flight for the squadron but good training for me. I was glad I made the decision to land when I did because the airport went below minimums, and we had seven inches of new wet snow within the next four hours. I thought about the flight as I drove home on the hazardous snow and icy roads. I felt like a guinea pig and still wonder, *Why do I find myself in these situations?*

I HATE COLD PIZZA

It is a routine practice for fighter squadrons and almost every other organization in the United States military to practice recall procedures to muster the organizations in response to possible emergencies. This narrative is a personal event while I was a pilot in the 191st Interceptor Squadron, UANG.

During this time, I was married with two young children, was a full-time student at the University of Utah, a fully qualified interceptor pilot in the 191st Squadron, and worked full time for the local telephone company. I worked in a company garage in downtown Salt Lake City from four o'clock in the afternoon until 12 o'clock midnight, Monday through Friday, servicing vehicles.

While I was getting ready to close the garage and return home, I received a telephone call stating that the 191st Interceptor Squadron was activating a recall exercise, and I was instructed to report to the squadron at the Salt Lake City Airport. It was not a lengthy drive from my work to the airport, so I was one of the first pilots to arrive.

I was instructed to suit up in my flying gear, preflight my assigned F-86L, and stand by for possible scramble. Paired with another pilot and formed in a standard flight of two aircraft, we received a scramble order. We made our takeoff time within the five-minute goal and enjoyed a night intercept mission against each other.

After landing, I was instructed to leave my parachute and helmet in the airplane and get ready to scramble again after being refueled, if needed. Sure enough, about 2:00 a.m., I was scrambled again and repeated the experience of the first flight. At least I was obtaining nighttime which helped fulfill my quarterly requirements.

After landing from the second flight, some of the other pilots suggested we order some pizza. We had worked up an appetite running to the airplanes and flying in the middle of the night. We all chipped in some money to cover the cost and were told the delivery would be within a half hour.

Well, guess what? I was scrambled for my third flight of the night before the pizza arrived. While I was gone, the remaining pilots enjoyed nice warm pizza but did save me a couple of pieces. When I landed, I was tired and hungry, so I hung up my parachute and helmet and was told I had flown enough and to stand down.

I sat down to relax and to eat my pizza. By then it was cold, and we had no way to heat it. One of the pilots said he liked cold pizza, so I began to eat. I always thought pizza should be served hot, and eating cold pizza did not satisfy me one bit. After about half a slice, I quit and threw the rest of my share of pizza in the garbage.

Finally, the exercise was called off. We had done a good job and were released to our homes. I barely had enough time to get home, change clothes, grab a quick bite of breakfast, and get to the University for my 7:45 a.m. class.

I do not mind flying three times, but *I hate cold pizza.*

Cold pizza

CHAPTER 5

★

Everett, Washington

C-119 FLYING BOXCAR

I know what you are thinking: *What is this kind of plane doing in a jet fighter pilot's war stories?* I do not talk much about this, but it is a part of my aviation experiences. Well, it fits right into the title of this book.

When I graduated from the University of Utah, I was hired by the Boeing Airplane Company in Seattle, Washington. As a result, I had to leave the UANG. However, I wanted to continue my part-time flying with the air force. Fortunately, I was able to transfer from the UANG directly to the Air Force Reserve without losing any time and at the same rank. Even though it was closer, I probably could have transferred to the Naval Reserve at Sandpoint Naval Air Station, but I did not want to be in the navy.

The AF Reserve unit was the 97th Troop Carrier Squadron in the 349th Troop Carrier Wing, Continental Air Command. The squadron's home base was Paine Field, Everett, Washington, a few miles north of Seattle. It was a comfortable drive from our home in Bellevue, Washington. The obligation was identical to the ANG with one Saturday and Sunday mandatory "drill" each month. We also got paid for twelve additional "drills" each quarter. For pilots, it was a way to stay current in an airplane. I was not the only new guy. There were three others new to the squadron. Their former experience was all in multiengine aircraft. My experience was all in single engine jet aircraft where I was the only crew member. In the C-119, the basic crew was the pilot in command, copilot, navigator, and loadmaster.

Fairchild C-119 Flying Boxcar

I had to swallow my pride to go from a jet fighter to an old airplane with two reciprocating engines and a mission of carrying people or freight instead of being "at the sharp end of the spear," so to speak. The C-119's primary mission was to carry paratroopers to a drop zone and have them jump out. The back of the fuselage opened, so it was easy to have two columns of troops jump connected by a static line that opened their chutes as they departed. In my entire few months in the squadron, we never dropped a single parachutist but did haul people and cargo.

Our training consisted of a few hours of ground school to learn the airplane systems, capabilities, and procedures. I spent as much time as I could in and around the airplane to learn where everything was and what they did. Finally, we started to fly. Since all of us new guys were being trained to be "pilots in command," we sat in the left seat and the instructor taught us from the right seat where a copilot would usually sit. We could start, taxi, takeoff, fly, and land the airplane from either seat. The cockpit instruments were archaic. The heading indicator even had to be reset periodically to the magnetic compass. Everything was powered by electricity or vacuum.

I was glad to get back in the air and rapidly remembered how to start reciprocating engines. Taxiing was like any other airplane without nose wheel steering but had a wider wingspan so the pilot had to make sure there was clearance from hangers, parked aircraft, etc. My checkout went smoothly, and I was certified as a copilot and soon upgraded to pilot in command. Of the four of us who began training together, I was the only one to be certified to fly the left seat as pilot in command. The others were copilots. There was some "heartburn" when we flew together, and they had to be my copilot.

Two mission flights are memorable to me. The first was to carry about twenty-five educators from Seattle to Colorado Springs for a visit to the AF Academy. It was winter, cold, and in clouds all the way. Peterson Field at Colorado Springs was below minimums for landing. The pilot in command said we would have to return to Paine Field and abort the mission. I said, "Let's try an alternate." Pueblo Airport and Buckley ANG base were also below minimums. My pilot was ready to turn toward Washington. I said, "Let's try Denver's Stapleton Airport as a last resort." It was a low ceiling, but *okay* to try. He flew an instrument approach and landed safely. A phone call to the academy got buses on the way for our passengers, and the mission was successful. It showed that fighter pilots are more aware of contingencies, look for alternate solutions to problems, and think way beyond the existing situation; I proved it that day with a very seasoned and experienced C-119 pilot who had no knowledge what alternates there were nor how to save the mission.

While we were living in Bellevue, Washington, Patsy had our third son on October 2, 1962. On October 29, our squadron was activated to support the Cuban crisis. We did not deploy anywhere but were on active duty at Paine Field. I took a military leave of absence from Boeing.

The crisis only lasted a month, and we were tasked to fly from Everett, Washington, all the way to Key West, Florida. I was assigned to fly copilot and enjoyed the very long cross country. We spent a couple of nights there and loaded the airplane with ground equipment from the fighter squadron that had been deployed from MacDill AFB (Tampa, Florida) to Boca Chica Naval Air Station at

Key West. Our job was to return it to MacDill and then go home. It was a long trip with a lot of flying time at 180 knots (207 mph) and good weather all the way. I also got to spend the night at MacDill and visited old friends that I knew previously in Salt Lake. My total time logged in the C-119 in the few months I flew was pilot, 67.5 hours; copilot, 40.9 hours = total 108.4 hours. One benefit from this experience was it added a multiengine rating on my civilian commercial pilot license.

Since I was on active duty, I put in a request to remain in the air force and not return to Boeing. I just wanted to keep flying. My request was subsequently approved, and I was given orders to transfer to Langley AFB, Hampton, Virginia. That assignment brings me to the next story…so stay with me.

CHAPTER 6

★

Hampton, Virginia

CESSNA 310 "GOONEY BIRD" OR T-33

It was a long drive from Bellevue, Washington, to Hampton, Virginia, in February 1963. It was cold outside; the roads from Indiana east were covered with ice, and we arrived at our destination in a snowstorm. Langley Air Force Base was the headquarters of Tactical Air Command (HQ TAC) which owned the tactical fighter fleet. Now I was getting somewhere and could speak fighter lingo again.

I was assigned to the 4500 Air Base Wing. Our mission was to provide service to the pilots in HQ TAC to keep them current in an airplane and earn their flight pay. We had two sections of airplanes. On one side was the reciprocating, multiengine aircraft consisting of Cessna 310s, a C-47 "Goony Bird," and an H-21 helicopter. The other side was the jet section with twin engine T-39s and a large fleet of T-33s.

Since I had come from the C-119, I was assigned to the "recip" side and was told I would fly the twin-engine Cessna 310. I was not happy. I asked for an audience with the boss over both flying sections. He was Lieutenant Colonel Watts, and I was a first lieutenant. I took my form five (pilot's flight log) and showed him I was really a jet pilot and had no desire to fly the slow airplanes. I proved that I had over two hundred hours in the T-33, over six hundred hours in F-86s, and only one hundred hours in the C-119. I wanted to be in the jet section. Convinced, he reluctantly made the change, on a trial basis, and challenged me to prove myself so he would not regret taking the chance on me. Whew! The first battle was won, and I was as happy as a clam.

This assignment turned out to be very beneficial. First, I was made an instructor, a standardization evaluation check pilot, a training officer responsible for approximately 180 pilots in HQ, and a functional check pilot (maintenance test pilot). I usually flew two times a day grading proficiency or instrument evaluation flights or checking out a new pilot in the T-33. I also flew several cross-country flights all over the US. The first year, I logged 550 hours in the T-33. I cut back to 450 hours the second year. The air force required two evaluations a year, and I always received very high grades. I worked hard and did my best. I wanted the boss to be happy with his decision to assign me to the jet section. I fit in well even though I was the lowest rank pilot in the section. However, I had senior pilot wings which proved I was an experienced pilot.

I enjoyed many personal experiences in this assignment. I became a better instrument pilot because of all the bad weather we "enjoyed" at sea level on the Chesapeake Bay. Landing at Langley AFB, we frequently saw the cloud ceiling at two hundred feet with a half-mile visibility. On every test flight, I performed both left and right spins just to make sure less proficient pilots would be able to recover if they went out of control for some reason; spins were not required on the test card because nobody intentionally spun jets. I also got to fly as copilot in the T-39 with my boss, Major Norm Schmidt. The T-39 had two jet engines and was only used to transport the HQ TAC high-ranking officers. Acrobatics were not approved maneuvers in the T-39, but we flew a couple of aileron rolls just for fun. Of course, we never told anyone about that part of the test flight.

North American T-39 Sabreliner

I flew as copilot in a C-47 "Gooney Bird" with a friend in the reciprocating section. The airplane was almost as old as I was but was still used to carry people and cargo. It was a fun experience, and its slow speed only enhanced my love for jet fighters. I also got to fly a helicopter (H-21 "Banana") just for fun. I was not very successful trying to hover in place, and I never flew another "whirly bird."

Douglas C-47 Skytrain, "Gooney Bird"

Another highlight of that assignment was when I was asked to go to the Massachusetts Air Nation Guard to check out two pilots as instructors in their T-33 support aircraft. It was a two-week job. Their primary aircraft was the F-86H. It had a much bigger engine (9,600 pounds of thrust compared to 7,500 pounds of thrust in afterburner in the F-86L) than the models I had previously flown and was a very "hot" jet. My brother-in-law, Major General (MG) Larry Killpack, had flown it and spoke very highly of it. I bargained with the squadron commander and the AF advisor to let me fly the H model before I left to go back home. I flew it twice one day after I certified the T-33 instructors. It was a blast.

The first flight was to become familiar with flight characteristics. I took off with my instructor in another F-86H chasing me. I made turns, flew acrobatics, pulled five or more Gs, and finished by making three landings. My second flight was dogfighting the squadron standardization evaluation check pilot. I won the fight and went home a very happy fighter pilot again.

After two years, I felt it was time to move on. I discussed it with my boss, and he sent me to his boss with whom I had bargained to be assigned to T-33 jets. Scared about being turned down, I found Lieutenant Colonel Watts to be very receptive. He said I had done an excellent job, and he was happy with his decision to let me fly the T-33. He inquired of my desires.

The F-4 Phantom was the newest fighter at the time, but it had two seats with a pilot and a weapons system operator (who was also a rated pilot) in the back seat. I had already flown to MacDill AFB where the first two wings to get the F-4s were located. I met with BG Albert Schintz, the division commander. He said he would take me, but when I asked if I would be in the front seat, he told me that, at my rank, I would start out in the back seat. That did not appeal to me, so I did not request the transfer with TAC personnel supervisor as BG Schintz suggested.

I told Lieutenant Colonel Watts that my first choice was to fly the F-104C Starfighter at George AFB, California. It was the fastest airplane in the AF, had one seat, and was the envy of every pilot that ever saw it. Lieutenant Colonel Watts told me to go to our wing headquarters and see the director of personnel. I went immediately but was nervous because every pilot wanted to fly the F-104. I did not know the guy I was going to see and considered going to HQ TAC personnel and talk to the boss with whom I had previously flown and had a friendly relationship.

When I knocked on the door, the major behind the desk invited me in. I sat down and introduced myself. He hesitated for a moment and said, "So you want to go to George AFB and fly the F-104." Obviously, Lieutenant Colonel Watts had called him with a heads-up. I thought it was all over before we even got started until he said, "I think I can help you with that assignment." Instantly, he became my "best friend," and I did not even know him. We worked out the details when I could get packed, household goods shipped, and travel time driving cleared across the country. Incidentally, my wife was eight months pregnant with our fourth son. It was my big chance to become a fighter pilot again.

Everything worked out well. I flew to George AFB and found a house to rent in Apple Valley. A few weeks later, we drove out of Hampton, Virginia, in another snowstorm. It was February 1965. Incidentally, my wife was pregnant with our fourth son who was born thirty days after we arrived in California.

Postscript: My first boss at Langley AFB was Major Norm Schmidt, and we became very good friends. Coincidently, Norm was also reassigned to George AFB in the F-104 about a year before I was. When I got to George AFB, our families occasionally got together for dinner, and we grew to be close friends. In 1966, Norm and I were in the same squadron at Udorn, Thailand, for my second combat tour. He was not my flight commander, but we chatted every day until he was shot down on September 1, 1966, over North Vietnam. Norm was captured and became a prisoner of war POW) until, one day, he was taken out for interrogation and beaten to death. He left his widow, four children, and many of us who knew him well. Fortunately, Norm's body was returned to the US in 1973 when the prisoners were repatriated. He was promoted to Colonel and was awarded the Air Force Cross for his bravery as a prisoner.

GO FLY AN L-19

After I talked my way to the jet section at Langley AFB, I was busy flying an average of ten flights a week. It was great. I met many people, added a lot of hours to my pilot log, and enjoyed a wonderful historical part of our country with my family. Langley was the home of TAC HQ. There were many kinds of practice exercises all over the command simulating actual war-type situations. It was good training because exercises replicated situations that could happen somewhere in the world.

Eglin AFB, Florida, was a prime location for many exercises. It was utilized continually. I don't remember what the exercise was called or what the goals were, but it was the period of time when our involvement in Vietnam was escalating. As a result, pilots were assigned to participate in the exercise as forward air controllers (FACs). The job was to fly an L-19 and direct the attacking aircraft to specific targets. That sounds exciting; however, the L-19 "Birddog" had two seats in tandem and flew at an "eye-watering" speed of 110 knots (125 mph) and, seldom, more than two or three thousand feet above the ground.

I did not volunteer to go but thought it might be fun to learn to fly a different kind of airplane. I was secure in returning to my jet job, so why not go to the Florida Gulf Coast for a couple of weeks.

By the time I was asked to go to Florida, packed, flew to Eglin, settled in a room, and learned where everything was located, the exercise was in the last scheduled week. I reported to the lieutenant colonel in charge of the FACs on Monday. He did not know I had been sent there and told me they could not check me out in the L-19 until Wednesday.

A light went on in my head. I responded that I did not know what it took to check out in the L-19, but even if I was qualified on Wednesday, that only left two more days of the exercise. My question to him was, Would I even be used, and was it cost effective to be trained in the airplane? He thought for a moment and realized it was a waste of time and money and that I might as well return to Langley. I was back with my family in time for supper.

Cessna L-19/O-1 Bird Dog

The subject came up again a couple of years later after I was reassigned from Langley AFB to George AFB. We arrived at George AFB in February 1965. I was fully qualified in the F-104 Starfighter by June, had logged one hundred hours in the airplane, and departed to Da Nang, South Vietnam, on July 8, 1965. We were sent to fly combat missions for the next few months.

By September 3, I had flown thirty-three combat missions in the F-104. Our assistant operations officer was Major Iwo Kimes with whom I had a "cool" relationship. I was the lowest-ranking pilot (due to slow promotions in the ANG) in the squadron, but I was not the least experienced pilot. Nevertheless, he treated me like a new guy even though I was fully qualified in the airplane and was a certified flight leader after five combat missions. I was equal to anyone in the squadron.

Iwo scheduled me to fly with a FAC in the back seat of an O1-E Bird Dog (basically an L-19) on an actual combat mission. He thought this would be a broadening experience since we occasionally worked with them on some of our air-to-ground weapons delivery combat missions.

I was not happy and tried to argue out of the flight but to no avail. As a fighter pilot that flew hundreds of miles per hour, I did not want to get shot down in a puddle jumper one thousand feet above the ground and flying at 80 knots (92 mph). My mental picture was of a sitting duck.

I sat in the back seat wearing a flak vest and sitting on another one...at my request. We flew west of the Ashau Valley looking for potential targets. I had them give me an M-16 rifle and several clips of ammunition, so we had some defensive firepower. Whenever we saw tunnels or anything else interesting, I fired the M-16 at them.

I guess I showed Iwo by making the little airplane into a fighter by firing my gun at suspected enemy locations. I also logged my thirty-fourth combat mission but was happy to fly all my subsequent combat missions in the F-104.

CHAPTER 7

★

Victorville, California

STARFIGHTER PILOT

We left Hampton, Virginia, in February and took the southern route. Leaving Raleigh-Durham, North Carolina, we finally drove out of snow and icy roads. I told the family that I had rented a house in Apple Valley, California. Curious, they asked me what it was like. I kept making comparisons when I told the family to look at the fields and said, "Apple Valley is kind of like this except not as green." I had not told them that we were going to live in the Mojave Desert. It was a nice house with a lot of desert around us. There were other homes in the neighborhood, but they were scattered apart, so we had no next-door neighbors. We "enjoyed" a lot of sand, cactus, scorpions, black widow spiders, and burrs that destroyed bicycle tires.

The 479th Tactical Fighter Wing had three squadrons: the 435th, 436th, 476th. I was assigned to the 436th Tactical Fighter Squadron. I signed in upon arrival anxious to get started on my checkout in the F-104C Starfighter—my dream airplane. I was still the lowest ranking pilot in the squadron. I soon discovered that there were a lot of "prima donnas" flying the F-104. Why not, it was sleek-looking and the fastest airplane in the air force. It would go twice the speed of sound (Mach 2) in level flight. Also, there was no training school for this airplane like they had for the F-100, F-105, and F-4, which were the other frontline fighters. I would get a squadron checkout just like I had with the F-86E.

1st Lieutenant Harold Alston, Starfighter pilot

We had a few two-seat F-104Ds to fly before getting to the tactical weapons deliveries, air refueling, and simulated air-to-air combat flights with the single seat "C" models. The T-33 that I had been flying was a good transition airplane because the height above the runway and visibility from the cockpit were almost the same as the F-104. The big differences were the takeoff and landing speeds. I really had to speed up my thinking from 120 knots (138 mph) on final approach to 175 knots (201 mph). It took a couple of flights to get my brain caught up to the airplane, but I consciously got it done. From then on, the checkout was fun and progressed quite quickly.

I flew my first flight in an F-104 on March 1, 1965. Four flights and four landings later, I flew my first "C" model (single seat) with my instructor, Captain Roy Blakeley, my flight commander, chasing me in another airplane. Because of my previous fighter experience, I progressed quite rapidly. I flew every day except on March 19, 1965, when our fourth son, Rodney, was born in the George AFB hospital. I was back in the air the next day however.

Lockheed F-104C Starfighter

I passed my transition evaluation flight on March 26, 1965, and passed my combat ready evaluation on May 25, 1965. I was fully qualified in air-to-air refueling, air-to-ground strafing, skip and dive bombing, air-to-ground rocket delivery, air-to-air gunnery, and fired an AIM-9 heat-seeking missile. What was even better was that my name was on the wing gunnery board for having the most accurate scores in rocket delivery. I was competitive in the other events. Not bad for the rookie of the squadron, eh!

20mm and air-to-ground rocket head

On July 8, 1965, we departed George AFB via a C-135, and after three stops, we arrived at Da Nang Air Base, South Vietnam, on Sunday, July 11, 1965. I had one hundred hours in the F-104 by then and flew my first combat mission the next day.

I kept a journal of my combat experiences in another book so I will only make a couple of observations here. My flight commander, Roy Blakeley, who checked me out in the F-104 was killed on July 22, 1965. It was my tenth combat mission. We do not know if he was hit by enemy fire, but his left wing leading-edge flap separated and ricocheted to the left side of the fuselage that caused a large hole. I joined on his wing in seconds and reported the aircraft damage. Roy said his oil pressure was dropping. That was a significant problem. I flew formation with him to Chu Lai Naval Airbase which was the closest emergency landing site. The runway was constructed of pierced steel planking, and Roy skidded off the runway into a sand dune and exploded. He was killed instantly and became our first casualty. That was a real combat baptism by fire, but it would not be my last.

It was a very sad loss to the squadron and to me personally. I met with his family when I came home and told them he was my hero and tried to console them in their grief. Several years later, I received a telephone call from Larry Blakeley, Roy's son. We had a lengthy and wonderful conversation. Larry was very eager and happy to hear me tell him many of my experiences with his father. Combat memories never fade.

DART TOW... PLAN AHEAD

After coming home from Vietnam, I returned to normal flying almost every day at George AFB. I was not an instructor, but I was given an additional task not given to every pilot. I became a qualified dart tow pilot. The dart was a triangular shaped target pulled 1,500 feet behind an airplane. The purpose was to practice air-to-air gunnery by shooting the gatling gun with real bullets to hit the dart. It was great practice simulating shooting an airplane. The dart was not as large as an airplane but was an adequate target.

The 20 mm ammunition was not the same high explosive incendiary ammo we used in combat but had the same basic ballistics. We loaded tracers every eighth position in the ammunition belt so we could see where the bullets were going. Bullet tips were dipped in different colors of paint with a specific color loaded into each aircraft. When a bullet hit the dart, it left a colored hole.

The dart was covered with heavy foil attached to four wood "wings." Bullets hitting the dart just made holes unless they hit the wood structure. The dart target would usually last through four fighters making two or three passes each. After the mission, the tow pilot jettisoned the dart on the range where the range officer could count the hits. Matching holes and colors, he verified hits by specific aircraft. It only took one hit to qualify in air-to-air gunnery.

During taxi, takeoff, and climb to twenty-five thousand feet, the dart was carried on the left wing in a pylon-mounted carrier. Nothing was on the right wing, so it was not a symmetrical configuration. On the range, the dart was released, reeled out until the end of the cable, and was fully deployed. It was aerodynamically stable as it was pulled along at 350 knots (402 mph).

For safety reasons, the tow plane flew an elliptical pattern in level flight. The tow pilot gave a "cleared to fire" order when starting a thirty degree banked turn and ordered a cease-fire just before rolling level. The pattern was repeated at the other end of the track. No shooting was allowed at the dart with the tow plane in straight and level flight. Fighters flew a typical gunnery attack starting from a high "perch" turning toward the target, reverse the turn to acquire the dart, lock on with the radar calibrating gun sight, tracked the target, and fire the gun with the "pipper" (aiming reference dot) on the dart within 3,500 feet. The last thing was to break away at one thousand feet, to the outside of the turn, and climb back to the "perch" for another pass.

The tow pilot was invaluable because he controlled the entire mission. Occasionally, a pilot lost sight of the tow plane. It was incumbent on the tow pilot to get everyone in the proper position to avoid midair collisions, etc. I guess that was one reason why I was chosen for the additional duty. I had about the best eyes in the squadron and could see the F-104 at greater distances than the average pilot. It came in handy more than once.

One particular tow mission, I took Captain Jack Kwortnik in the back seat. It was his first flight in an F-104D after being assigned to our squadron as a new pilot. The mission went well, and we started back to the base. On the way, I explained to Jack that the dart tow rig would not allow landing with full flaps because they would hit the rig and damage the flap. As a result, landings had to be made using "takeoff flaps" with only thirty degrees down instead of forty-five degrees as in normal landings. Therefore, instead of flying final approach at 175 knots (201 mph), the speed would have to be 195 knots (224 mph), and the drag parachute would be deployed after landing below 185 knots (213 mph). We would use most of the runway just to get stopped.

I pitched out and on downwind told Jack that I would land close to the end of the runway instead of one thousand feet down just in case the drag chute failed. I was exactly on speed on final approach, touched down where I wanted, held the nose up until decelerating to below 185 knots, and pulled the drag chute handle. It was a great, unintended demonstration because everything I told Jack happened. The drag chute failed, I used as much aerodynamic braking possible before using the aircraft brakes so I would not burn them out or blow a tire. I was able to safely stop the aircraft using the entire ten thousand feet runway and turned off at the end to taxi back to the parking ramp.

The lesson learned is to always plan for contingencies. You never know when things can be different than what you expect. I guess the "aviation gods" were just testing me.

BOMBS AWAY

The F-104C had the ability to go to war with several capabilities. We carried an AIM-9 Sidewinder, heat seeking missile on each wingtip and two on a launcher mounted under the fuselage. However, we never used the latter missile launcher because it caused too much drag in combat situations. We had an internal Gatling gun that fired 20 mm ammunition of three different types. The first is practice ammunition. The bullet head is steel and only made a hole. This is what we used on the practice range when we strafed (fired the gun) a vertical ground target. The second is a tracer bullet that has a pyrotechnic in its base that could be seen when fired. It was most useful in air-to-air gunnery practice and actual combat. It was usually loaded every eighth round so the pilot could see where the bullet stream was going. Hopefully, it showed a course directly to the target or enemy aircraft. Small corrections could be made, if necessary, based on the visual trajectory of the tracer. We used tracers in practice on the dart air-to-air target and in combat. The third ammunition type is high explosive incendiary (HEI). We only used this type in combat. It was highly effective in destroying a ground or airborne target. I did not have the opportunity to fire HEI at enemy aircraft, but I caused a lot of damage strafing ground targets.

The aircraft also had a pylon station under each wing and under the fuselage. On the wings, we carried 750 pound general purpose bombs, napalm, or pods that fired 2.75 inch "Mighty Mouse" rockets from each pod. I delivered all three types of ordinance on many targets in combat. There were two items that we could carry on the centerline station. One was a two thousand pound simulated nuclear bomb of which I only carried one for a training delivery. In a dire time of need, we could carry an actual nuclear bomb. Fortunately, that was never required during the cold war with the Russians.

The last item that could be configured was a centerline mounted practice bomb dispenser. We carried it every day when we practiced weapons delivery prior to our combat deployment. It was aerodynamically shaped and could carry six practice bombs that could be released one at a time. It allowed us to simulate napalm delivery (skip bombing) and simulate real bombs delivered from a thirty-degree dive. The practice bombs only weighed twenty-five pounds.

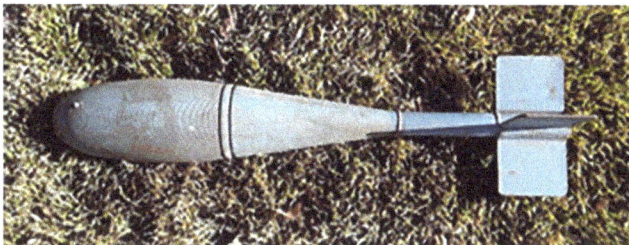

BDU-33 Practice Bomb

On a typical "bomb-rocket-strafe" practice mission, we were loaded with two rockets, one hundred rounds of 20 mm ammunition, and six practice bombs, two of which were for low-level skip bombing and four for dive bombing. We always flew in a flight of four aircraft to maximize range time and spacing while making our individual ordinance deliveries on the targets.

One particular day, I was scheduled to fly the number 2 position on the wing of our squadron operations officer, Major Eusebio Arriaga; we just called him "Seb." He and I had not flown together before, so he was probably evaluating my formation flying as well as my weapons delivery techniques and scores. I don't remember who the other pilots were in numbers three and four aircraft.

The procedure entering our Cuddyback range was in normal formation. I was on the left wing, and the other guys were on Seb's right wing. As we lined up entering the range, it was required to move the formation from "fingertip" to "right echelon" which meant that I had to cross under Seb to his right wing because we would break to the left at five seconds intervals to get individual spacing for our ordinance deliveries. The last thing was to open the dispenser doors so that the bombs could individually drop each time we depressed the bomb-release button on the control stick.

Seb dipped his wing to the right signaling me to change sides. At the same time, he gave us the order to open the bomb dispenser doors. An immediate thought came to me: *I don't want to cross under Seb when he opens the dispenser doors*, so I did not move. I saw his doors open and guess what? Just as I had pictured, a twenty-five pound steel bomb fell out. If I had crossed on Seb's signal, I would have been a perfect target for the falling bomb.

Where it would have hit my airplane I don't know, but it could have been in the windscreen, in the engine intake, or any place that would have done damage. It could have been disastrous. Satisfied nothing else was going to fall out, I made my cross-under and notified Seb that he lost a bomb. We continued with a routine training mission and enjoyed good practice.

In recalling this flight, I ask myself, *Why do I find myself in these situations?*

WING COMMANDER'S WINGMAN, PART 1

While I was in the 479th Tactical Fighter Wing, I had two wing commanders. The first was Colonel Darrell Cramer. I knew him quite well because we belonged to the same church. He was an elder, and I was the Elder's Quorum president. He was also very cordial to me on the base. I had the privilege of flying his wing from Da Nang Air Base (AB), South Vietnam, back to George AFB, Victorville, California.

Our route home included landings at Kung Kuan AB, Taiwan, Guam Island, Honolulu, Hawaii, and finally at George AFB, California. We were returning seven F-104s home from Da Nang AB. The first leg went well and was the shortest flight. Taiwan was where our major inspections were accomplished and was manned with our own maintenance personnel from George AFB. I had previously flown there and had stayed a week for periodic aircraft inspections and to fly a maintenance test flight. We had a good meal, a restful night's sleep, and close inspections of each airplane before our next leg over the Pacific Ocean.

The second flight was to Guam where we cruised with the KC-135 tankers so we could air refuel at the appropriate times and locations. They also did the navigating. All we had to do was fly loose formation. As I burned fuel, I noticed that my left tip tank stopped feeding and was about three quarters full. It was not worrisome but was annoying. It required constant trim to keep the wings level. I also had to refuel from the tanker a couple of extra times because of the trapped fuel that was not usable. I did not mind the additional refueling because the air was smooth, and it gave me something to do on the long flight.

Upon landing, I told the line chief about my problem. He said "not to worry." He had a solution, and I was able to continue with the scheduled flight. His fix worked fine from Guam to Hawaii (seven hours and forty-five minutes). So far, so good!

The last leg from Hawaii to George AFB was probably the most critical because there are no islands in that part of the Pacific Ocean on which to land in the case of an emergency. The flight plan called for more frequent fuel replenishments from the tankers. We had to keep enough fuel in case of an abort back to Hawaii before passing the "equal time point" (ETP). Likewise, after the ETP, our only option was to make it to Oxnard, California, if we did not have enough fuel to get all the way to George AFB.

Guess what? My tip tank stopped feeding again. Now it was a bigger concern because of the distance over water with no place to land. The normal schedule called for five air-to-air refueling over that part of the Pacific Ocean. I needed to refuel ten times and ignored the fact that if I had a problem, there was a stretch of several miles of ocean where I could not have returned to Hawaii nor make it to Oxnard. Needless to say, I was very proficient in air-to-air refueling. The only lasting problem was that I completely wore out the thumb on my right-hand flying glove because of so much trimming.

I made it to "feet dry," which is the common term for flying over land instead of water. The story is not over because the landing was still ahead. Colonel Cramer radioed my friend and fellow pilot, Captain Dave Clardy. He was riding in the tanker as the emergency contact during our ocean crossing. Colonel Cramer asked him to research my problem in the technical manual. The answer was to jettison the tip tanks. I thought that was unnecessary and a waste of the tanks, not to mention that the left tip tank was still full of fuel and could start a fire on the ground.

As we got close to George AFB to make our final landing, the boss (Colonel Cramer) suggested that I move to number 7 in the flight and make a straight-in landing after the other six had landed. I moved to the end of the formation but asked to be in the close formation flying the initial approach to the runway. Our families were waiting for us on the ground. The seven-airplane formation would look impressive, and I wanted to be part of it. Besides, I thought I could control the aircraft without problems.

Everything was normal with seven of us in right echelon formation. Each aircraft "pitched out" in five second intervals, including me. No problem, until I rolled out on downwind and was decelerating. The nose dropped a bit in the turn, and I was decelerating faster than normal. I engaged the afterburner to control my speed better and flew a longer pattern as Colonel Cramer had suggested in the first place. My longer final approach gave me plenty of time to trim, stabilize the roll of the airplane, and make a good landing. I was on the ground safely and taxied to the fuel pit in front of the squadron. Patsy and our four sons were waiting to welcome me home.

My problems were over, and someone else had to make a permanent fix to the airplane. Hugging my family after returning from my first combat tour was worth every concern and worry. And, oh yes, even wearing out the thumb on my flying glove from trimming so much.

Postscript: Colonel Cramer was from Ogden, Utah. As a member of the Pioneer Flight of the National Order of Daedalians located at Hill AFB, Ogden, Utah, it is our responsibility to select and maintain the Utah Aviation Hall of Fame. A brigadier general when he retired, Darrel Cramer was selected by us as the 2003 inductee into the Hall of Fame. As is the custom, we hosted a dinner honoring him and his family. I was able to renew our friendship, reminisce about our flights across the Pacific Ocean in 1965 and the friendship we developed even though we were separated by several ranks. He always treated me well and seemed to look after me in several ways. He occasionally stopped to chat when he passed our house on his way home and saw our boys and me playing on our front lawn. He was a good man, a good commander, and a true patriot worthy of being inducted into the Hall of Fame. He died a year later.

WING COMMANDER'S WINGMAN, PART 2

The previous story is the only experience flying with Colonel Cramer. This one is about flying with my second wing commander, Colonel Donald Ross. After my first combat tour at Da Nang, I was promoted to Captain. I was not an instructor but was a fully qualified pilot in all tactical events including flight leader. Colonel Ross wanted to become qualified in air-to-air gunnery and shoot at the dart target. He was scheduled as number 3 in the flight, and I was assigned to be number 4 on his wing. My job was to fly fighting wing and instruct him in procedures and the proper and safe gunnery pattern while firing the gun. He did a good job in all respects, so I did not have to coach him very much. It was fun for me to fly fighting wing formation while he fired the Gatling gun at the target.

Usually, we would only have a chance for two passes each because of the tow plane's fuel endurance. Major Charley Ward was leading the flight and called a hit on the dart on his first pass, so he pulled up and sent in number 2. I do not remember who that was, but he flew his two gunnery passes and called off also. Colonel Ross was next. His first two attacks were good, but he did not get a hit, so he was ready to pull off and let me fly my own patterns for a shot at the dart.

The tow pilot relayed to us that he only had enough fuel for one more shooting pass before he had to return home. Colonel Ross said he would pull off so I could get one shooting pass of my own. I radioed back for him to make another pass to try and get a hit, and I would make a pass from my chase position as he pulled off. *Pretty generous of me*, I thought.

From fighting wing position, just like combat, Colonel Ross flew his pass, did not get a hit, and pulled up and away. I stayed on the pass, got in range, and fired my Gatling gun. Bullets hit the dart hard and foil flashes could be seen by the other pilots who were watching my pass. Mission over, we headed for the base. It was successful for me and continued my qualification in air-to-air gunnery with that single pass.

After landing, Colonel Ross walked with me to the squadron, thanked me for instructing him, for my suggestions, and for my generosity giving him an extra attack. He complimented me for hitting the dart from my supporting position. It made an impression on him, and I appreciated his praise for my being his wingman.

Later, we deployed the squadron from George AFB to Myrtle Beach, South Carolina. It was to participate in a close air support exercise with the marines. Our squadron commander Lieutenant Colonel Harlan Ball led the flight; Colonel Ross was number 3, and I was his wingman again as number 4.

Since we were going nonstop, we had KC-135 tankers to refuel us halfway across the country. It was the first time for Colonel Ross to refuel in the air in the single seat F-104, and I was again his wingman "coach." I liked flying his wing again because he was a good pilot.

There was another benefit for my being in the first flight. As we prepared to join with the tanker, the radar controller called its position. Lieutenant Colonel Ball replied "no joy," meaning he did not see the tanker. Our join up was going to be a disaster if he did not get visual contact. I could not wait any longer and called "tallyho" (visual contact) at about eighteen miles. I gave Lieutenant Colonel Ball directions to adjust our course, hoping he would see the KC-135 and make his own adjustments. After a few more directions, he finally saw it at about four miles as the tanker turned for us to join behind it and to get in proper position for the refueling. Without help, our leader would have missed the rendezvous, and we would have been all screwed up trying to get back into position.

Colonel Ross did a good job refueling without any coaching from me, and everything turned out well. I enjoyed being his wingman again. I could not say the same for the squadron commander who was leading our flight.

Postscript: Colonel Ross had combat experience in World War II where he shot down a German aircraft and flew through the debris damaging his own aircraft which resulted in his parachuting to safety. He was captured and spent the next sixteen months in a German prisoner of war (POW) camp. He retired from the air force as a major general in 1974.

STARFIGHTER VERSUS PHANTOM

I was at George AFB during a time in Tactical Air Command when there was no dissimilar air combat training (DACT) allowed. We were allowed, however, to fight against each other in like airplanes, but it was considered too dangerous to "fight" other fighter types. As fighter pilots who might have to fight against Soviet MIGs, we considered it absolutely necessary to have experience against dissimilar aircraft to broaden our capabilities. I guess there had been too many previous incidents that caused commanders at various levels to avoid problems that air fighting different types of airplanes might cause.

At George AFB, we had two fighter wings. We flew the F-104C, and the other wing flew brand new F-4Cs. Our airplane was single seat with one pilot. The F-4C had a crew of two: a pilot in the front seat and a pilot or navigator in the back seat to operate the radar and other equipment. George AFB was a perfect place to gain experience in dissimilar air combat training.

McDonald Douglas F-4C Phantom

Captain Tom Delashaw was the 479th Fighter Wing Weapons Officer. He had been trained for his job at the formal Air Force Weapons School at Nellis AFB, Nevada. He was considered by all of us as one of the most experienced and knowledgeable F-104 pilots in the air force. Unquestionably, he was a great fighter pilot.

I do not know if there was an approved plan from Tactical Air Command to have a trial experiment with the two wings partici-

71

pating, but somehow, one was planned. Captain Delashaw coordinated with the F-4C squadron to provide airplanes and crews for the mission. He was tasked to formulate a plan, establish rules of engagement, brief, and lead the mission, schedule both squadrons for a debriefing and document observations and conclusions after the exercise.

The scenario was two airplane elements of both airplane types to take off and fly to different points in the air-to-air practice area (Death Valley, California). Both elements would level at twenty-five thousand feet. When an element had contact, they could maneuver to obtain lethal position and simulate shooting down one or both "enemy" aircraft. It was obvious that each airplane type would use their most advantageous capabilities to obtain a simulated lethal shot of missiles and/or guns. I should mention that the F-4C only carried missiles and did not have a gun for close-in fighting. Our F-104Cs carried sidewinder missiles on the wingtips and a 20 mm Gatling gun in the left side of the nose.

I don't know how or why, but I was chosen to fly on Tom's wing in this exercise. I was a captain and a new guy in the squadron, but I was fully qualified in all phases of the F-104 mission, had a lot of flying time, and had previous fighter experience. At any rate, I did not argue and was excited to fly the mission. I knew two things going into the flight. First, I could fly proper positions as well as any pilot in the wing in both close and combat formations. Second, I had proved to have as good or better visual acuity than anyone in the squadron and could see airplanes at longer distances. After looking at small silver F-104s, I figured that looking for larger and darker F-4Cs should be easier. Also, if they were not in afterburner, they left a black smoke trail from their two engines. To their credit, they had search radar that was supposed to find targets as far as twenty-five miles away. I did not think they could detect two F-104s at anywhere close to that distance because of our small profile.

We approached our meeting point from the south, and the F-4s approached from the north in a head-on engagement. We were on the same radio frequency, and there was no ground radar monitoring the mission. I spotted the F-4s at thirteen miles and called "tallyho at twelve o'clock, slightly high." They had not seen us on their radar. Already we had an advantage. Tom began our attack by going into afterburner, lowering the nose to accelerate faster, and began a sweeping turn to their six o'clock as we climbed to slightly below their altitude. Since I was in combat formation on Tom's left wing, he selected the lead aircraft on the right side, and I took the wingman. We made simulated Sidewinder missile passes, called the shots on the F-4s, and turned toward home still in afterburner and supersonic. The F-4s turned toward us, but we outran them, and they could not get an effective shot at us. We landed and logged about forty-five minutes of total flying time. It was a real "hit and run" flight.

The next phase of this exercise was the debriefing with both squadrons participating. Tom led the discussion. The F-4 crews complained that we did not fight fairly. Tom explained that the small wings of the F-104 would not allow us to turn with any other aircraft including the F-4. Our fighting tactic was to hit and run and avoid any kind of a turning fight. It was disappointing to the F-4s because they would have had the advantage in a turning fight. We made our attack, got our simulated shots, and escaped without having to defend ourselves.

There were several lessons learned. The F-4 is easy to see. Their radar did not acquire us until we had seen them visually. That was another "eye opener" to the F-4C crews. Pilots need to know the advantages of their own aircraft, and the disadvantages of enemy aircraft. Don't get "suckered" into a fight that might be fun but that you cannot win. It is better to fight and run away and live to fight another day than to fight when you are at a disadvantage.

When General Wilbur Creech was Commander of Tactical Air Command (1978–1984), he incorporated DACT in every fighter wing, instigated exercises where it was practical, and turned the tide from timid defensive aerial combat to an aggressive offensive force that was the best in the world. I am glad I served during this time and witnessed the changes in air force fighter capabilities. As commander of the 65th Fighter Weapons Squadron (Aggressors) at Nellis AFB, Nevada, I flew against almost every combat aircraft in the air force and navy and some foreign countries.

Postscript: We became well acquainted with Tom and his family at George AFB, California. He and his wife had two sons and one daughter. My sons and I took their son Tommy camping with us. He fit right in and was a cute, well-behaved boy. Tom had a distinctive career in the air force with two combat tours in Vietnam. After retirement, he flew F-104s in air shows with a civilian company in Florida. He also flew other aircraft. When ferrying a British Hawker Hunter, jet fighter, from Florida to Montreal to deliver it to a new owner, he refueled at Wilkes-Barre/Scranton International Airport, Pennsylvania. On takeoff, he had catastrophic engine failure and was killed in the crash on July 22, 2003.

CHAPTER 8

★

Da Nang, South Vietnam

MIGS

I admire air force aces. An ace is someone who has destroyed five enemy aircraft. I knew quite a few aces and flew with several of them. The following are just some examples:

- Ray Greenwood destroyed seven German aircraft in WWII, but they were on the ground.
- John Voll shot down twenty-one Germans in WWII. He was also the smoothest and most precise pilot I have ever flown with.
- Cliff Jolly had seven MiG kills in Korea.
- My boss at the AF Academy, Robin Olds, had sixteen kills: twelve in WWII and four in Vietnam.
- Steve Ritchie got five MiGs in Vietnam.
- Alden Rigby shot down five in WWII.

I could name many more with whom I flew who had air-to-air victories but were not aces.

I never got a chance to shoot at any MiGs in my 136 combat missions, but this story recalls the only enemy aircraft I ever saw.

My good friend, Donnie Tribble and I were assigned to escort a C-130 electronic intelligence "spy plane" over the Gulf of Tonkin east of North Vietnam and South of Hainan Island. Hainan was a Chinese communist possession. I was the flight leader, and we joined with the "Silver Dawn" aircraft as the C-130 was called. Our altitude was thirty thousand feet. We were significantly faster than Silver Dawn, so it required a weaving pattern of constant turns. We needed to keep the C-130 in sight, maintain combat maneuvering speed, and still scan the sky for possible enemy aircraft.

About halfway into the mission, we spotted condensation trails near Hainan Island heading for us. We turned toward them hoping to engage. They were MiG-17s. I thought to myself, *This might be my chance to get a kill.* I will take one and give the other one to Donnie. When we got closer to the MiGs, they turned back over Hainan. We returned to Silver Dawn because we were not allowed to enter Chinese airspace. The MiGs reversed their course and came toward us again. We turned back toward them, but they returned to the island. I knew they were trying to draw us into their airspace so they could try to shoot us down or that antiaircraft guns and surface to air missiles (SAMs) could try to shoot us down. I wasn't worried about fighting an MiG-17, but I did not want to dodge SAMs.

MiG-17 "Fresco"

We had already lost one F-104 with Captain Phil Smith when he experienced a heading indicator malfunction combined with clouds covering the Vietnam coastline and became disoriented. As a result, he was close to Hainan Island and was shot down by MIGs. He ejected and spent the next seven years in a Chinese prison.

I was not going to take the bait of their trap, so we returned to our mission and let the MiGs enjoy flying in their own airspace. Donnie and I safely completed our task escorting Silver Dawn and returned to Da Nang.

I summed up our mission with the MiGs as "No Runs, No Hits, No Errors" but reported our experience to the intelligence officer in our debriefing. I never saw another MiG. I was disappointed I did not have a chance to shoot down an enemy aircraft let alone become an ace. However, Donnie and I did accomplish the job we were sent to do.

GULF OF TONKIN SAMS?

The title made me scratch my head in disbelief. Who ever heard of surface to air missiles (SAMs) being a threat from the ocean? Nobody that I know. We had several missions to protect the C-130 Silver Dawn. I introduced this type of mission in the last story. It was not very exciting but was a time builder and usually took more than three hours requiring refueling in the air a couple of times. The day before, I flew the first mission of the day and was supposed to be relieved by another flight that was scheduled for second mission. Unfortunately, they aborted, and my wingman and I had to stay and cover the entire time. That flight lasted six and a half hours. I was tired after four hours.

The day after that long flight, I was back doing the same thing. We had code names to warn us about threats from SAMs. It was a boring flight until we received the code over the radio from the Silver Dawn (C-130). We were too far away from any known SAM site at Haiphong. We were also too far away for a launch from Hainan Island and knew the Chinese would not fire at us in international airspace.

SA-2 surface-to-air missile (SAM)

I rolled upside down and looked at the Tonkin Gulf below us. I saw nothing coming toward us. Having seen no missiles, I searched the Gulf again. The only thing I saw were a few boats of various sizes and design. I assumed they were North Vietnamese fishing boats and that none were American because our navy did not go that far north. I tossed off the threat to some false electronic phenomenon, but I did appreciate the warning just in case.

At the conclusion of our mission, we returned to Da Nang Air Base. As usual, we sat down with our intelligence officer for our mission debriefing. We discussed the normal mission items and had no tactical items to report. Then I mentioned the SAM warning while over the middle of the Tonkin Gulf. I commented that it did not make any sense to me even though we took it seriously at the time and found that no missiles were fired.

The intel officer asked us to wait a minute while he retrieved a book. He opened it and showed us a picture of a small ship. I told him that it could have been one of the boats I saw when I was searching the water. His response was that they had heard of a boat capable of firing a SAM but had never had any confirmation. He said it was probably an enemy boat that was testing its "fan song" (SAM) radar.

I was not happy that intelligence guys had this knowledge and did not pass it on to us. We were flying in the area where it could have made a difference. It was not the first time they failed to brief us on possible threats, and it would not be the last. I have another story to write about intelligence information that fighter pilots should have been given but that were kept secret in the intelligence section vaults. "Yikes guys," let's cooperate. We are on the same team.

REFUELING BASKET

Jack Gale and I flew together on my forty-fourth combat mission. It was a routine escort mission over the Gulf of Tonkin, and we needed to refuel twice with a KC-135. When we rendezvoused with the tanker for our last air-to-air refueling, there was a flight of F-105s ahead of us. They needed fuel to return to their base in Thailand. Usually, they refueled using the tanker's boom (the "pipe" that transferred jet fuel from the tanker to the receiver) that plugged into the fighter's receptacle. The boom operator, on the tanker, maneuvered the boom into the receptacle while the fighter was stabilized in position. F-105s also had a retractable probe so they could refuel on a drogue (a basket on the end of the boom) configured tanker. They were not used to using the probe and drogue system as it was more difficult. The tanker did not have the ability to change from one to the other. It was configured before takeoff for one or the other system depending on the type of aircraft they would service. The F-105s needed the fuel to get home, so they had no choice but to use the probe. It showed by the trouble they had in trying to hook up. One of the pilots must have been new because he really beat up the drogue trying to get engaged. Our F-104Cs had a fixed probe, so we could only refuel on a drogue-equipped tanker.

KC-135 Refuels an F-104C

Jack went first but abruptly disengaged from the drogue. He reconnected and got his fuel without any additional problem. Then it was my turn. I slid into position and approached the drogue. My contact was good as I placed my probe directly into the center of the drogue. It sounds pretty good, doesn't it? Well, it wasn't. The tanker boom operator (the "boomer") started fuel flowing. With the diameter of the hose (about five inches) and the pump pressure, we could take on three thousand pounds of jet fuel in about five minutes. This time, when the fuel began to flow, the basket broke off the hose and remained attached to my probe.

I was surprised but not overly worried about it unless it, or pieces of debris, fell off and entered my intake. If that happened, it would take out the engine, and I could never make it to a runway. The thing that startled me was the hose was pumping fuel directly into my left intake which was just below the probe. I felt a shudder and saw the engine instruments jump. The exhaust gas temperature indicator went way above normal. I backed away and pulled up to avoid any additional raw fuel going through my engine.

I glanced at Jack, and even with our oxygen masks covering our faces, I think our eyes showed the bewilderment we felt. We dropped below the tanker, and I radioed that I was heading for Da Nang Air Base. The last I saw of the tanker, fuel was still spraying out of the hose. I am sure that the "boomer" was as shocked as I was. Jack stayed on my wing and asked how my engine looked. Everything was back to normal. He reported that fire shot a hundred feet out of my exhaust, and he thought my engine had blown up.

Getting close to Da Nang, I declared a precautionary landing straight into the runway. Jack stayed with me at a comfortable chase position until I landed safely. I taxied to my parking spot and saw the bewildered look on the crew chief as I shut down the engine. When the word got around to the squadron, everyone had to come and see what strange equipment I had brought home. The pilots joked that I was a real "ham fist" (a pilot who is rough on the controls) until Jack explained that I was a victim of circumstance, and my flying technique was not in question.

After landing with refueling drogue

We kept the basket in the squadron briefing room and considered using it as the base for a podium. I had no way to keep it and did not want to ship it home. After all, it was military equipment. I do not know what happened to it. I can swear on a Bible that I never saw nor heard of a similar incident, before or after, in the numerous times I refueled in the air. *Why do I find myself in these situations?*

TALLY-HO, THE TANKER

This is another combat mission with Jack Gale. I was the flight leader, and Jack was my wingman. It was another long escort/MiG combat air patrol mission that required air-to-air refueling. We completed the first phase of the mission and turned south over the Gulf of Tonkin to rendezvous with our KC-135. They were restricted from coming too far north where they could be threatened by enemy fighters or SAMs.

Our join up with the tanker was coordinated with a combat surveillance radar facility located near Da Nang. As we headed south and the tanker flew north, the controller called out periodic positions for us. At our first contact, they advised us the KC-135 was at "eleven o'clock and seventy-five miles." We were also separated by a thousand feet in altitude. The standard geometry was to fly head-on until about twenty miles away. At that distance, the tanker made a 180-degree left turn. If all went well, the fighters would be a mile or so behind the tanker and just flew into formation on its right wing.

The day was perfectly clear and the water below us was calm. With a day like that, a common term for fighter pilots was that "you could see clear out of sight." As we continued to fly closer, additional cues were transmitted to us. When the controller called "eleven o'clock at fifty-two miles," I saw a tiny black dot and called "tallyho." Looking over to Jack, he was shaking his head. I knew he was thinking that no one can see an airplane that far away regardless of its size. Also, it was not even leaving a condensation trail.

As we got a little closer, Jack called "tallyho." The controller responded that our distance was now forty-four miles. It was probably the easiest join up I ever made. We got our fuel and returned to our mission in the north.

After we completed the mission and landed at Da Nang, Jack commented that he did not think it possible to see an aircraft at those distances. However, when he personally saw it at forty-four miles, he knew I was honest in seeing the tanker when I had called it.

Jack spread the word about the great visibility on the mission and bragged honestly about the ranges at which we got visual contact on the KC-135. From that time forward, the members of our flight admitted I had the best vision; hence, they wanted to fly my wing or have me fly on their wing because I could see airplanes at greater distances than they could. Besides, it might come in handy if we were over North Vietnam when the MIGs were flying. Maybe we could

WHY DO I FIND MYSELF IN THESE SITUATIONS?

spot them before they could see us. That would be our advantage. Unfortunately, we never saw enemy aircraft on subsequent missions. I did see a lot of friendly aircraft before my fellow pilots, so there were some benefits to having good vision.

Postscript: Jack Gale and I were very good friends. We were stationed together at Langley AFB, George AFB, Da Nang AB, and Luke AFB. He retired as a lieutenant colonel and returned to Williamsburg, Virginia, with his wife, Jeanne, and their two sons. Years later, I sent a letter for his scrapbook celebrating his eightieth birthday. He died a couple of years later. Jeanne died from a fall, at home, two or three years after Jack. I am thankful for many great experiences in the air and with our families on the ground.

THE WRONG INITIAL POINT

One of the fun benefits of flying high-performance fighter jets is that one minute you are flying at thirty-five thousand or forty thousand feet, and the next minute, you might be at five hundred feet above the ground. The closer to the ground, clouds, or anything else that provides a reference of speed, the more impressive it is when flying fast. Speed is not the subject of this story but a foreword to what comes next.

In the F-104, we trained to fly low-level navigation from an initial point (IP) to a specific destination such as a target. Some flights might require several turns or course corrections and may require minutes or even an hour to fly from point A to the planned finish. Speed is another factor. For convenience, the F-104 was comfortable at 420 knots (483 mph) which is seven miles per minute. We also used 480 knots (552 mph) or eight miles per minute and as high as 540 knots (621 mph) or nine miles per minute. The higher speed requires higher fuel flow, so endurance is important. Also, hostile defenses might require a faster ingress to keep an element of surprise and make it more difficult for an enemy to hit a fast-moving target at a very low altitude. Finally, at low level, you cannot see other significant identifiable features unless they are quite close to your route. To be successful, you must be very accurate controlling heading and speed; otherwise, you can wander off course or be early or late over checkpoints and mess up your whole low-level flight.

We were scheduled to hit a target in North Vietnam. Our armament load was two 750-pound, general-purpose bombs on each of our four aircraft in the flight. Iwo Kimes, our assistant operations officer, scheduled himself to fly with our flight in the lead position. I was the most junior officer in the flight but not the least experienced and was positioned as "tail-end Charley" (number 4 in the flight).

Before the briefing, I studied the map and rehearsed in my mind how I would plan the flight. Iwo briefed that we would fly at 500 feet and 420 knots (483 mph). Each aircraft would drop back five hundred feet from the aircraft in front. This allowed enough separation, so we did not have to fly close formation, presenting a bigger target for the enemy and allowing each of us to navigate on our own.

The initial point was a bridge over a river in the southern part of North Vietnam. It was an excellent place to begin because it was easy to find and was a perfect location to start the clock. Ideally, if the planned route were flown from checkpoint to checkpoint at precisely 420 knots, then at the precalculated total elapsed time, each of us would climb high enough for a thirty-degree dive angle delivery. At the apex, the target would be acquired, and the dive delivery commenced.

All would have gone perfectly except for one thing. In laying out the route, Iwo failed to notice there were two bridges over the river exactly seven miles apart. He chose the second, more northern bridge as the IP. As we passed the first bridge, Iwo called to "hack" the clock to begin our time to the target. I knew it was wrong but did not say anything. Neither did other members of the flight.

The low-level part of the flight was perfect, but at the preplanned elapsed time, Iwo radioed that he did not see the pull-up point or the target. I immediately transmitted, "Continue for sixty more seconds." The time went so fast that Iwo did not respond but did what I suggested. He saw the correct final check point, popped up for his delivery, and put his bombs on the target. Three of us followed his lead and hit the target as well. Whoopee, target destroyed.

We surprised the enemy with our attack, but as we turned to egress out of the area the "bad guys" began to shoot at us with their 37/57 mm antiaircraft guns. Being smart pilots, we dropped to ground level, accelerated as fast as we could, and outran their attempts to do us harm. None of us got hit.

After landing at our debriefing, I showed Iwo where he made the mistake selecting the wrong bridge and how close together they were. He was not happy with my pointing out that he hacked the clock on the wrong IP and responded, "I think you give yourself too much credit." I turned the other cheek and did not argue. After all, I was a first lieutenant and Iwo was a major, but unknown to him, our fighter pilot experience was not dissimilar. I did not want one of our squadron leaders to look bad to the other guys, but I knew I was correct, and that he screwed up.

Postscript: This is a humorous side light to the mission described above. I mentioned that the bad guys were shooting at us as we completed our bombing runs and started to egress. Every man was on his own until getting over the South China Sea and away from enemy guns. Then we rejoined in close formation and returned to our base.

I was the last one to drop bombs, so the bad guys knew what to look for. I knew I was the most vulnerable as the closest and last aircraft attacking the target. From a thirty-degree dive-bomb pass, our pull-out was about one thousand feet above the ground. I did as I was trained, but when I saw the guns shooting at me, I quickly descended as low as I dared. The terrain in the immediate area was mostly flat and dotted with rice paddies. The profile of an F-104 was very small, so I pointed my tail directly at the gun battery. That gave them a very small target. I also lit the afterburner and accelerated to supersonic speed to get out of the area as soon as possible. I did not look anywhere except straight ahead because I was only five feet, or less, above the terrain going over 646 knots (760 mph).

I outran the guns, but out of the corner of my eye, I saw a North Vietnamese, probably a rice farmer, standing on the edge of a paddy. I flew by him about fifty yards to his side going over Mach 1 (speed of sound). The "loud boom" caused by the shock wave coming off the aircraft was very loud. I was sure it scared the poor "Gook." I was not going back to see if he was still standing, but in the many years since that day, I have often wondered what his reaction was to my foreign aircraft, being an enemy to his country, the loud noise of the engine, the "sonic boom," and if the shock wave blew him off the dike. I will never know, but while the desire to know fades, the vivid memory of the wild experience never has. I still wonder if the shock wave knocked off the dike into the wet rice paddy and if he had any hearing loss from the boom. Oh well, it makes for a good true, but humorous, end to a dangerous combat mission.

NEW "CLUB" MEMBERSHIP

There are a lot of clubs to which we can belong. They might be book club, athletic club, bridge club, bike riding club, hiking club, hunting club, dinner club, etc. You may belong to some type of club as you read this.

Well, the club I will tell you about is just a little different because there is only one prerequisite to belong. This club never meets for lunch nor to renew friendships. In fact, precious few of us even know who the members of this club are. Finally, it is very selective about who can be accepted into this auspicious group of people. If your curiosity is peaked, just read on.

On September 1, 1965, I was the spare for a flight of four. When one of the aircraft had problems, I was scrambled and joined the flight to fill in where the aborting aircraft had been. I became number 3 in the flight and led the second element. The mission was fighter escort over the Gulf of Tonkin and the eastern part of North Vietnam. It was my thirty-third combat mission.

It turned out to be a routine mission that included refueling three times from a KC-135 tanker. We usually only refueled one or two times, but we had to cover a longer period that day. The weather where we flew the mission was good. However, on our return to Da Nang, the report was low clouds with constant rain.

The bad weather required us to fly a ground-controlled approach (GCA). Under radar control, we began our descent into the dense clouds. I made sure my wingman flew close formation and planned for us to land in formation, which was routine, and got us on the ground as fast as possible. There was other traffic that would be recovering behind us, and I did not want to have them delay their landings any longer than necessary.

Stabilized on downwind of the rectangle-shaped pattern, we followed the headings and altitudes assigned us for the approach. My wingman was in excellent position, and I flew as smoothly as possible to make it easier for him despite occasional turbulence.

The final leg of the approach aligned us with the runway. We could not see anything except rainy clouds in which we were enveloped. I, of course, just looked inside my airplane at the instruments to maintain exact headings, altitude, and airspeed. With only a few miles to go, I was instructed to begin our descent.

The glide slope angle (two and a half degrees) required about 650 feet per minute in the descent. With precise directions from the radar controller, we approached from north to south toward the ten-thousand-foot runway. Using hand signals, I motioned for us to lower the landing gear and flaps. We decelerated to our normal final approach airspeed.

Finally, not more than a mile from the end of the runway, I began to barely see the end of the runway and continued visually to a routine landing. Thanks to the radar controller, he had aligned us perfectly, and the glide slope placed our landing about a thousand feet from the end of the runway.

I took the right side of the runway, and my wingman landed on the left side. There was about four inches of water on the runway. With that much standing water, I knew we would hydroplane until we decelerated enough for our tires to touch the pavement where light braking would become effective. Under these conditions, it would be impossible to stop without using our drag parachute. Looking in my left mirror, I saw my wingman's drag parachute come out of the tail compartment. It "blossomed" normally, and he decelerated nicely under the circumstances. I made sure he had a good chute and could safely stop in the distance remaining. I deployed my drag chute at about 165 knots (189 mph).

Unfortunately, my chute did not blossom open. It must have been wet, twisted the risers, and offered no decelerating help. I used brakes sparingly to not swerve and run off the runway. I declared my problem and advised the tower and my wingman that I was going to engage the barrier to stop. I dropped the tail hook, and it contacted the cable perfectly at about 90 knots (103 mph). It saved me from going off the end of the runway into a muddy field.

The barrier engagement worked exactly as it was designed and stopped me about five hundred feet from the end of the runway. I let the cable tension pull me back enough so the maintenance crew could disengage the hook from the cable. That done, I taxied to my parking spot still dragging the hook.

My engagement with the barrier was reported to the cable manufacturer, E. W. Bliss Company. They sent me a certificate, suitable for framing, and a wallet card certifying me a member of the Grand Order of Tape Dragons. Membership is exclusive for pilots who have stopped their airplane with the aid of Bliss Company's lifesaving cable device.

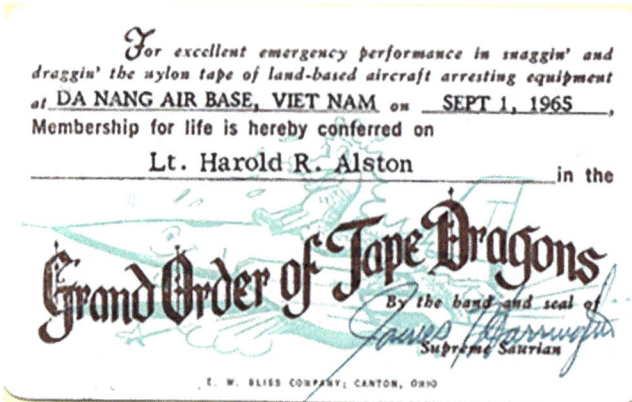

Tape Dragons wallet card

As a member of this selective "club," I have never attended any meetings, am not acquainted with other members, and not a minute has been wasted with "tea and crumpets."

It certainly trumps a bridge club, doesn't it?

Postscript: Maybe you have experienced hydroplaning in standing water while driving your automobile on a freeway or a highway with a high-speed limit. You can compute the speed at which this dangerous problem will occur. The formula is *nine times the square root of the tire pressure.*

Example: Tire pressure = 36 psi (pounds per square inch)

The square root of 36 is 6. 9 x 6 = 54. So *54 mph* is the critical speed at which you will hydroplane standing water on the freeway.

Remember, your automobile does not have a drag chute to help you stop, so be prepared.

CHAPTER 9

★

Udorn, Thailand

FIRST SAM SIGHTING

I flew sixty-one combat missions while at Da Nang Air Base in 1965, and I never saw a SAM. While we flew a lot of missions over North Vietnam, not too many were in the Hanoi area. The only SAM launch sites were ringed around Hanoi, and there were only seven of them. That changed when I went back to the war flying out of Udorn Royal Thai AB in Northern Thailand. Hanoi was still protected by the original SAM sites, but additional sites multiplied to over 150. They were not all manned, but the radar control trailer and launchers were mobile and could be moved to other prepared sites. Also, the inventory of missiles had greatly increased with the help of the Russians and Chinese. We did not worry about SAMs in the southern part of North Vietnam because none were based there. The northern part of the country was a significant worry because SAM sites were everywhere, especially around Hanoi.

My squadron flew F-104Cs that had no radar homing and warning (RHAW) equipment. We flew a lot of support missions with F-105s (nicknamed "Thuds") that were equipped with RHAW equipment. They could detect when enemy radar became active, when a missile was launched, and the direction from which it was coming so that evasive action could be taken.

Two of our squadrons had already served in combat in 1965. The 435th squadron was scheduled to deploy to Udorn, Thailand, in 1966. Patsy and I discussed why it might be advantageous for me to volunteer to transfer to the 435th so I could return to combat and complete a full tour. Otherwise, I was certain that with only sixty-one previous missions, I would be sent back in some less desirable capacity. The normal tour of duty in the war was one year or one hundred combat missions over North Vietnam. She agreed that the sooner I went back, especially in the job for which I was trained, the sooner I could return home. I volunteered, and my transfer was gladly accepted.

To prepare the way for the squadron, an advanced group of fourteen pilots, eight aircraft, and several maintenance men were to be sent to Udorn two months before the main squadron would arrive. The wing asked for volunteers. I volunteered immediately (with Patsy's permission, remember) to guarantee going early. Nine of the fourteen pilots were to only stay two months and then return home. The other five of us were to remain and train, orient, and make the transition easier for the squadron when they arrived. It was a big responsibility, but I was up to the challenge because I had been promoted to captain, was already a combat veteran, and would fly several more combat missions before the squadron arrived. When we were at Da Nang, we were on the South China Sea. We would now be west of Vietnam, in Thailand, and would fly all our missions over Laos and North Vietnam. Udorn was the most northern base from which United States Air Force (USAF) aircraft were based. This gave us the advantage of getting to the targets sooner and endurance to remain longer.

The day came for the deployment of the advanced party. Since I had flown an ocean crossing the year before, I was not chosen to be a primary pilot. Only the temporary duty pilots, who would return home when the main squadron arrived, would fly this ocean crossing in the opposite direction. However, I was scheduled to fly a spare aircraft in case one of the primary aircraft had problems and had to abort the flight. We had four spares that took off with the main flight. Numbers three and four flew to the first refueling position (over the

91

Pacific Ocean), received fuel, but were not needed so they returned to George AFB. Howie Sargent and I flew to the second refueling, received fuel, but again no one aborted. We were more than halfway to Hawaii by that time, so if any primary aircraft had problems, they would have to continue. Not being needed, we turned around and headed back to California. It required us to refuel one more time returning to our base, so a KC-135 tanker came with us to give us enough fuel to safely fly home. After more than five hours in the air, looking at blue waters of the Pacific Ocean, we basically went nowhere and landed where we took off at about 6:00 p.m. Howie and I had flown a longer flight than the eight primary aircraft going all the way to Hawaii.

We parked the airplanes, repacked our bags with our parachutes and helmets, took a bathroom break, called home for a few minutes, and then jumped on a C-130 and headed back toward Hawaii. We finally landed in the middle of the night. It had been a long day. I appreciated the speed of the F104 because I had flown twice as far as the C-130 in half the time. At least I could "catnap" in the back of the "trash hauler" (a fighter pilot's term for a cargo carrying airplane) and leave the job to others to get us to Hawaii.

The rest of the trip was uneventful, and we arrived at Udorn the day after the fighters landed from their long flights from George AFB. Now we could go to work. Our squadron was replacing the 555th (triple nickel) Tactical Fighter Squadron of the 8th Tactical Fighter Wing which had been relocated to Ubon, Thailand. They flew the F-4C Phantom. A small group had remained at Udorn to orient us as to locations, missions, and everything else they could think of to prepare us for the new missions we would fly. We teamed up with them and flew with an F-4C leading and an F-104C as wingman. It was a pretty good mix because the F-4C had a crew of two with long range radar and missiles for armament. Our F-104Cs only carried one pilot but had a 20 mm Gatling gun in addition to missiles. Our speeds and endurance on the missions were about the same. It did not take long to get oriented to flying over Laos (where the air-to-air refueling tanker tracks were) and to become acquainted with the significant landmarks in North Vietnam. You could not miss the Black and Red Rivers, Hanoi, the northwest and northeast railroads, Haiphong Harbor, Thud Ridge, etc. If we were over any of these areas, we knew exactly our position, how far it was back to Udorn, (about 350 miles), and the direction to fly to get us there.

It was my eighteenth mission flown from Udorn. We flew with the F-4Cs to escort two American B-66s and prevent enemy MiG aircraft from attacking them while over North Vietnam. The B-66's job was to monitor and gather electronic intelligence with very sophisticated on-board equipment. The B-66s were unarmed, so we were their sole protectors. Typically, the mission was at thirty thousand feet for about forty minutes in a very dangerous and highly defended area. We arrived before the strike package and remained until they egressed.

Douglas B-66 Destroyer

We established our orbit shaped like a horse racing track with two parallel flight paths on the sides and a 180 degree turn at each end. A B-66 was at each end of the track with an element of two fighters in combat formation. All went well during the mission. The Thuds successfully attacked their targets. There was quite a bit of action below us against specific targets and SAM sites. A couple of Thuds were hit with flak but not seriously.

The strike package had completed their mission and was heading home. I was glad we could finally go home. Then to my surprise, the lead B-66 said they were going to make one more circuit. Mentally, I almost came out of my seat. The mission below us was over. Why not also leave and get out of danger? Why tempt fate? Now, I was worried about doing something that seemed to me to be totally unnecessary, stupid, and risky. Adrenalin surging through my body indicated I was now scared. We were the only ones left in enemy territory. Guess who would get enemy attention now.

At the far end of our track, we turned back toward the west. There was only half of the track remaining, and we would go "home" to Udorn. Just as we rolled out, I saw two very fast "aircraft" pass to our right. I thought they were MiG-21s. I made a call over the radio, "MiGs, five o'clock." Then I realized they were not MIGs and corrected it to "They are SAMs." I guess nobody else saw them because there were no additional warnings except mine. They were the first ones I had seen but would not be the last.

I was still worried because the enemy usually fired three missiles in a quick volley.

Almost immediately, I visually acquired a third missile streaking toward us and hoped it would miss. I radioed "break" (a hard turn). Almost simultaneously the F-4 pilot also called "break." I knew it would miss us but wondered if the proximity fuse or the SAM controllers on the ground would detonate the SAM. It was a dangerous split second. The missile exploded underneath the B-66. I held my breath until I saw fire coming from the underside of the B-66. I responded over the radio, "You're on fire, eject." I saw the two ejection seats come out the top but did not see the bottom ejections. Finally, I counted four descending parachutes. I never saw the fifth parachute but later found out that they all made it, were captured, and were held prisoner until repatriated in 1973.

It was a tough mission, and lessons were learned. I never misidentified a surface-to-air missile again. Of course, after this experience, almost all my missile sightings were aimed at me. Oops, there goes the adrenalin again.

FLAK OVER THE ARCHIPELAGO

The 435th Tactical Fighter Squadron pilots finally arrived at Udorn Royal Thai AB to relieve the temporary duty (TDY) pilots who returned home. The handful of us from the 435th advanced party greeted the incoming pilots. It was our job to brief them on our squadron facilities, hangars, ramp space, base facilities, other residents, the town, air refueling tracks, possible target areas, and everything else that the new guys should know.

I was assigned to a flight commanded by Major Terry Cawley. On his first flight, he scheduled me to lead a flight of four with him as number 2—my wingman. The mission took us across Laos and Vietnam, refuel over the South China Sea, fly north to the Gulf of Tonkin, then turn west past Haiphong, North Vietnam, toward the Hanoi area. Our job was to patrol the area for enemy MiG fighters.

Crossing the coast at thirty thousand feet, I was impressed with the beauty of the country. The water was very blue, and off the coast was an archipelago of many small islands with lush foliage. It looked like a nice place for a vacation getaway. It had trees, beaches, water, and a pleasant climate. What more could one want?

I was jolted back to reality from my "pretend vacation" in the tropics when I saw numerous black explosions around us. My immediate thought was, *How dare they shoot at us and destroy the beauty of the country and the quiet peace we were experiencing?* I recognized the flak as 85 and 105 mm antiaircraft explosions like we used to see in newsreels from World War II. I took the flight through evasive actions and continued inland to our assigned area. Those big guns were not very accurate like the 37/57 mm guns that were radar-controlled. I was more concerned with SAMs being fired at us at that altitude. As we flew inland, a few miles, the flak ceased, thankfully. We continued our mission and devoted our attention to being vigilant for MiGs and SAMs. Surprisingly, over that very hostile area of North Vietnam, we were left alone, and no MiGs entered our area of coverage.

At the completion of our MiG combat air patrol mission to return to base, guess what? The bad guys again opened fire with their big guns, and we had black explosions all around us again. Now, I was doubly angry at them for destroying the peace of the most attractive part of their country. Obviously, it made no difference to them, and they failed in hitting us with their obnoxious flak.

I was glad that the mission was not too exciting for the new pilots that I had on my wing. It was, however, a very good orientation on combat refueling, the geography of the area, and getting shot at. I was sure the next time we flew together, it would be over a different location and more exciting for them. We all had to learn fast in everything we experienced. Every flight was dangerous, and something was always learned. The more we experienced, learned, and retained, the better combat pilots we became. I hope Terry and my other wingmen saw it the same way. They had a lot to learn.

SAIGON

The entire war in Vietnam, Laos, and other clandestine areas was managed by 7th AF in Saigon, South Vietnam. Our mission assignments, ordnance requirements, times over target, air-to-air refueling tracks, call signs, and everything came from 7th AF. Besides the permanent staff of officers and airmen assigned there, it was their practice to have representatives from the squadrons, who were carrying out their daily orders, come to Saigon. It was a TDY assignment for a week or two as a liaison officer to help plan strikes, act as an expert on specific locations, targets, aircraft capabilities, potential problems, and so on.

I knew I would have to go to Saigon and fill the liaison task at some time. Therefore, I chose when to go. After all, I had never seen Saigon before and thought it would be interesting and give me an edge on how the war was fought from a headquarters' point of view. I considered the planners as strategists with the big ideas of what, when, how, and who to execute the war. I am a tactician who plans and executes the orders from headquarters using our best tactics and capabilities for successful outcomes.

After being in Thailand and having flown five combat missions in six days, I volunteered to go to Saigon and get my stint as liaison over with. I flew from Udorn, Thailand, to Tan Son Nhut AB in Saigon, South Vietnam, as a passenger in a T-39 courier aircraft. My assignment was from the fifteenth to the twenty-sixth of June 1966. Our air force contracted quarters for us; liaison pilots were off the base at 190B Nguyen Min Chu in Saigon. It was hard to forget the address after staying there, even for a short time. The AF Security Police found a Claymore mine outside the building just the day before I got there. I thought to myself that I would be really angry if I got killed by a Viet Cong mine outside my quarters in Saigon instead of in my F-104 over a hostile target near Hanoi.

There were two houseboys who made our beds and cleaned the bathrooms. I slept with my wallet under my pillow. One morning, I got up and discovered my uniform belt and flight cap were missing. I was not happy because they were there when I went to bed. I approached one of the houseboys and told him I was very angry. I instructed him that the belt and cap had better be returned to my room when I came back from work or I would take care of them both. I would not tolerate being treated that way while protecting them from *their* enemies. On my return, later that day, I surprisingly found my belt and cap and had no more trouble with the houseboys.

My roommate was Captain George Peacock. He was the F-105 liaison officer from Korat AB, Thailand. He had been shot down a week or so before he ejected from his F-105 and broke his leg. It was in a full leg cast, so he could not even bend his leg. He woke up when one of the houseboys came in his room for his wallet. He yelled and scared him away without losing anything. We locked our rooms, but the boys had keys. George told the kid that I would kill him if he tried it again. That made me the bad guy, but neither one of us had any more trouble from them.

Since it was off base, we had to take a taxi to and from work. The taxi was a small Renault. It had a Vietnamese driver and two seats in the back. George could hardly get his tall frame and unbendable leg in the back seat. I gave him as much room as I could and helped position his casted leg to fit the space.

I won't describe details of our daily work, but we attended daily briefings, planned mission briefings to the director, BG George Simler, contributed our expertise, and approved the mission orders for the following day. One of the major missions we helped plan was a raid on the Hanoi petroleum, oil, lubricant (POL) storage facility. It was in a very heavily defended area, and we knew there would be losses from our attacking forces. The F-105s would do the bombing, and "my" F-104s would provide the MiG combat air patrol to keep enemy fighters off the bombers. I wanted to get back to Udorn and fly the mission that I helped plan, but it did not work out because I could not get a replacement before my ten days were up. I could not "leak" any information back to the squadron about the fifty airplanes (bombers, tankers, fighters, rescue, jammers, etc.) as well as our detachment's role in the dangerous mission.

There was one more serious incident George and I experienced. We took a taxi from HQ back to our quarters. On the way home, it did not seem to be the most direct route with which we had become familiar. I turned to George and said, "I do not think we are going the right way." He also had a frown on his face and agreed. When the driver turned in to an alley, we both became worried. I told the driver to stop, and we were going to get out. As we did, I saw a marine jeep with two military policemen coming our way. They knew we were in trouble and were being taken to a bad place. We got George in the jeep with his casted leg, and thankfully, they took us where we needed to go. It was comforting to see the guns on their hips. By the way, we did not pay the taxi driver.

During my off time, I visited the intelligence section and discovered they had a library with technical manuals on Soviet MiG 15, 17, 19, 21 aircrafts. We were exposed to encounter MiG-17s and 21s anytime we went north in the Hanoi area. None of us in the 435th TFS had any performance knowledge of these enemy airplanes. I asked the intelligence people why they did not disseminate the aircraft performance data to us who were faced with fighting them. Their answer was because "it was classified *secret*." My reaction was, "What good did it do nonrated intelligence people who would never see an enemy to have the classified data in a vault?"

They did let me review the manuals, and I memorized much of the performance data that could be important for us fighter pilots to know in possible dogfights. When I got back to the squadron, I briefed the pilots on the "secret" information I had gleaned from my time in the vault.

Postscript: Based on the low rate of USAF air-to-air victories against enemy fighters, it was not long after the Vietnam War that it was finally realized we needed training against dissimilar aircraft including captured enemy aircraft. Eventually, the USAF Aggressors were formed with F-5Es to simulate MiG-21s to fly enemy formations and tactics and expose fighter wings with tactics they could face in another war. Also, the secret (since declassified) 4477th Squadron, Red Eagles, was formed with MiG-17s, MiG-21s, and MiG-23s flying against our air force fighter and bomber wings.

My final base assignment at Nellis AFB, Nevada, gave me command of the 65th Aggressor Squadron for two years. I may not have shot down any MiGs in combat, but I certainly "shot down" (with film, not bullets) a lot of fighters and was also "shot down" by air force fighters. Our job was to train AF pilots how to fight MiGs if they ever had the opportunity in combat. Our goal was for our friendly aircraft to acquire skills and "shoot" us down. When they learned to win the air battle against the Aggressors, our work was successful. It was the best job I ever had in my twenty-eight years of the air force service.

LAST COMBAT MISSION

This narrative is not about the tactical portion of my one hundredth combat mission over North Vietnam but the return and landing which completed my combat tour of duty.

I was the leader of a flight of four, and our mission was obviously in North Vietnam but near the Laos border and south of Hanoi. The target was a storage area that included a cave. We were each armed with two 750-pound general purpose bombs to be delivered in a 30-degree dive. We had an airborne FAC who described the target and where he wanted our bombs to hit for maximum damage. I elected to make two passes dropping a single bomb each time. We accomplished the job without incident, and I felt really good about my last mission. With all the experience I had in dropping bombs, my last bomb hit directly in the mouth of the cave. My wingman, who saw it hit, complimented me on my accuracy. Bull's eye!

Following number 4's last bomb delivery, we rejoined in a loose formation to return the approximate two hundred miles to Udorn. We changed to the radar site's radio frequencies so they could identify us and provide information on possible traffic as we flew toward home.

Several times, they asked me to confirm our location and altitude as we progressed toward Udorn. I thought it was unusual, and it got a bit annoying because I knew where we were and where we were going. I did not need their help.

As we crossed the Mekong River, I had the flight change radio frequency to the Udorn control tower. I reported our location and that we were a flight of four. The control tower then provided instructions for the runway in use and the surface wind. On the initial approach, I told the flight I was going to go around, but they were all to land. When my wingmen were all safely landed, I requested a pass down the runway which was approved by the tower.

Since it was my last mission, I kept the landing gear retracted and accelerated to about 400 knots (460 mph). At the approached end of the runway, I performed a couple of aileron rolls the length of the runway giving the tower and my flight a little show to end my combat tour.

Having shown off enough, it was time for me to land. Rather than flying a standard initial approach, I came in low and performed a three-quarter roll to the right with a hard-left climbing turn to pattern altitude. As I did this little acrobatic maneuver, one of the pilots on the ground said, "Watch out for flying debris." I wondered what he meant until I looked quickly to my right and saw an F-102 who had been escorting me in close formation. I realized that I had rolled toward him before my acrobatic pitch up for landing; I did not know he was there. He had been sent up by my squadron commander to escort us home in celebration of my being the first pilot in the squadron to fly one hundred missions over North Vietnam. Now I understood why radar kept asking me our location and altitude. Fortunately, he was quick and was out of the way and avoided a mid-air collision. I continued my climb to downwind (1,500 feet above the ground), lowered the landing gear and flaps, flew a normal final approach, and touched down on the Udorn runway for the last time.

After parking my airplane, the F-102 pilot came over to meet me. I apologized for our near miss and admitted I did not know he was there as I concentrated on my little air show finale. Fortunately, everything turned out well, but future victory rolls were not allowed for completing combat tours. Also, I do not think F-102s were asked to escort anybody else on their final missions. *Why do I find myself in these situations?*

Convair F-102 Delta Dagger

CHAPTER 10

★

Phoenix, Arizona

A FAST TRIP HOME

While stationed at George AFB, Victorville, California, or any place where I was stationed, it was always fun to take an airplane and fly cross-country to a different base. With tongue in cheek, we said it was necessary to remain proficient in "navigational proficiency." The truth being told, it was to see a new location, experience a weekend of better weather and warmer temperatures, or to visit friends or family.

One weekend, I flew to Luke AFB, Phoenix, Arizona. This trip was to find a house for our family. Since Rodney was born at George AFB, California, we were now a family of six. Patsy and I decided we did not want to live on base. We had only moved on base at George AFB for convenience for Patsy while I was in Thailand. Now we wanted to relocate in a nice neighborhood, in our own home, where the boys could make friends and be established community citizens. Because I was a qualified F-104C pilot, my new assignment after my two combat tours in Southeast Asia was to Luke AFB. We were to report in January of 1967.

Luke had the F-104G. It would be no problem converting to a different model. The G model was the German version of the Starfighter, and Luke was the location where all German pilots were trained before they returned to Germany to active fighter squadrons. I would be an instructor pilot and fly almost every day. That is just what every fighter pilot craves, and I was no exception. It was going to be a great assignment.

I found a house to buy that would be perfect for our family. I had four bedrooms, two bathrooms, a nice kitchen, big living room, family room, and a two-car garage. The backyard was fenced, and there were three citrus trees: grapefruit, orange, and lemon. Wow. Those were three fruits that were frequently purchased at the grocery store. Now we could just pick them off our own trees. Best yet, the price of the house was affordable.

Having completed my business, I was anxious to get home and relay the news to our family. To milk the opportunity, I planned two flights with a landing at Nellis AFB, Las Vegas, Nevada, to quickly refuel before continuing to George AFB. I could have gone directly to George AFB from Luke AFB but wanted two flights…just for fun.

I also did not want to climb to altitude but decided to stay level at ten thousand feet and cruise at supersonic speed. The speed of sound (Mach 1) at sea level is computed at 68 degrees Fahrenheit, in dry air, to be 667 knots (768 mph).

I took off from Luke AFB and headed straight to Las Vegas at ten thousand feet. Since it is basically desert all the way, I accelerate to 1.1 Mach (624 knots or 734 mph). I did not fly over any small towns so they would not experience the sonic boom and made the flight, including acceleration on takeoff and deceleration before landing, in twenty-two minutes. By automobile, it is 286 miles from Phoenix to Las Vegas and took five hours.

I did the same thing from Las Vegas to Victorville and made that flight in thirteen minutes. An automobile would drive the 165 miles in three hours.

It was fun for me, but the crew chief was not happy when he saw that the insignia paint on the sides of the airplane was destroyed from the heat generated at Mach 1. I broke the sound barrier "jillions" of times but never again at ten thousand feet of altitude.

BOUNCE THE BOGEY... WOOPS!

Following my combat tours in Southeast Asia, I was posted to Luke AFB, Arizona, as an F-104 instructor pilot training German pilots. All their training was there because the flying weather and availability of practice ranges in Arizona were much better than in Germany, and experienced pilots, like me, were plentiful to be instructors. It was a great assignment. I was among many pilot friends I had known before, and we flew almost every day. It was a nice place to live, albeit hot in the summer. Finally, the Germans were pretty good pilots for being new to a very high-performance aircraft.

With a full day of numerous scheduled sorties, weather was always an important consideration. If sorties had to be cancelled, it would put students and the program behind schedule requiring flying on a weekend. Another solution was to add sorties, but that put a strain on the maintenance airmen who kept the airplanes in flyable condition.

There are times, even in the desert, when serious weather occurs. High winds, thunderstorms, blowing dust, overcast clouds, etc. You get the idea. We had to consider the experience, familiarity of the training areas, instrument capability, etc. to allow student pilots to fly and accomplish training requirements for specific training missions. Safety is always a huge consideration.

An aircraft was scheduled to check weather in all training areas for possible weather-related problems that could be a factor in the day's flying schedule. It was always a two-seat F-104, flown by two instructor pilots, taking off a couple of hours before the first scheduled training flight. Corollary to checking weather, the pilots could not only log the time, but they could accomplish individual requirements such as a back-seat landing, instrument approach, aerobatics etc.

My good friend and fellow instructor pilot, Mike Vivian, and I were scheduled to fly the weather flight early one morning. Mike made the takeoff, and we flew around the training areas which extended from Northern Arizona to the Mexican border and west to

California. The weather was great, and we reported it, by radio, to our squadron operations desk.

Since it was such a good day, we accomplished our mission in half the time for which we had fuel. Now we could play, and we certainly were not going to land early. We stayed north of the base while flying rolls, loops, Immelmanns, and hard turns at six Gs. After a few maneuvers, we both spotted a bogey (unidentified aircraft) north of us and a little higher than our altitude. Fighter pilots are trained to shoot down enemy aircraft, among other tasks. When we see an unidentified aircraft, they are fair game until identified.

I do not remember who was flying the airplane at the time, but we both had the same idea: go get it. Afterburner was engaged, and the nose was aimed at the bogey. Our plan was to intercept it with overtake speed from three thousand feet behind, in a right turn, and track it with the gun sight. It was a perfect gun attack just like we trained against the towed dart target with live ammunition.

As we got within a thousand feet lower and within a couple of miles, we both said whoops and rolled inverted, pulled four Gs, and hoped we had not been seen. Our bogey was an SR-71 Blackbird. It was a new high-altitude reconnaissance aircraft capable of Mach 3. It had recently been made public. Because the SR-71 was black, we had focused on it and did not see the KC-135 tanker, a couple of miles ahead, at the same altitude. Our bogey was closing to accomplish an air-to-air refueling test. Since we both had experience doing the same thing, we quickly escaped not wanting to distract the Blackbird pilot from a critical phase of his flight.

Lockheed SR-71 Blackbird

Lockheed SR-71 Blackbird Refueling

We landed after we had used most of our fuel. Neither Mike nor I ever told anyone we were the bad guys who almost interrupted a critical test with an almost secret aircraft. You won't tell anyone, will you?

AFTERBURNER BLOWOUT

It is always challenging for an instructor to fly his own air-craft and mentally fly the student's aircraft at the same time. A good instructor thinks way ahead of the present situation for possibilities of what could occur next. Those might include actions to be taken in case of an emergency, distance and altitude from a possible landing site, what the student is doing wrong that needs to be corrected, and so on. You get the idea. The instructor bears responsibility if the student has not been taught correctly or exceeds acceptable parameters for the objectives of the flight. The instructor is always mindful of safety for himself and for the student.

After many training sorties flying low-level navigation, weapons delivery, formation, and instruments, the syllabus had only one advanced lesson that was different from all the rest.

The aircraft configuration required two tip tanks, two underwing pylon tanks, all filled with fuel. On the centerline pylon was a bomb dispenser simulating a nuclear bomb. At that configuration, it resulted in the maximum gross weight of the F-104G at over twenty-six thousand pounds. As a result, the takeoff roll at Luke AFB, even at 1,100 feet elevation and a 10,000 foot runway was much longer than the pilots were accustomed to seeing. It was also the only time I flew the F-104 at maximum gross weight.

I briefed the student on the entire mission and gave him some tips regarding aircraft handling at heavy weights, especially on takeoff. On most missions, we took off in close formation. On the heavy weight flight, I briefed the student that he would takeoff first, and I would follow after a ten-second delay. His call sign was Rainbow Lead and I was Rainbow 2 (Rainbow was my personal call sign).

Start, taxi, and line up on the runway were normal. When we were cleared for takeoff, my student released brakes, engaged the afterburner for maximum power, and commenced his roll. After ten seconds, I began my takeoff.

F104 takeoff with afterburner

About the time I reached 100 knots (115 mph) and was accelerating normally, I looked at the student's tailpipe and saw his afterburner go out and the nozzles closed. I knew immediately it was an afterburner blowout, and there was no way he could take off in military power with the weight we were carrying. I brought my throttle to idle and called, "Rainbow Lead, abort, abort, abort."

My next instruction to him was to bring the throttle all the way back to idle, check his airspeed, and pull the drag parachute handle when below 180 knots (207 mph) and only use brakes in the last couple of thousand feet of the runway. I did the same thing. It was close, but we were both able to get the airplanes slowed enough to turn on to the taxiway at the end of the runway. The alternative would have been a barrier engagement, and I did not want both of us taking the barrier. I knew I could stop but had doubts about the student. He performed a very good abort under the existing conditions.

We did not successfully complete the briefed mission, but on the other hand, we both completed a perfect abort under bad circumstances. It was just another day in the life of a student and instructor pilot. Now you see what I meant about the instructor mentally flying both airplanes. It could have been a lot worse for the student without instructor promptings.

Our job is to teach them to know as much as we know so they can be the best fighter pilots that they are capable of being.

LOW LEVEL FLIGHT IN WEATHER

I know what you are thinking: *Low level flight in weather is just plain stupid.* You've gotta' be kidding me, right? Well, you would be correct, but read on for the explanation.

This also occurred at Luke AFB in the F-104 with a German lieutenant as my student. By this time, the student had completed transition, instrument, and formation phases which are in the syllabus. Now he was being introduced to tactical phases that would make him a qualified fighter pilot. This flight was at low-level, flying a navigational route at 500 feet above the ground at 420 knots (seven miles per minute) airspeed. It is fun but challenging because everything up to this point was done at medium altitudes, well above the ground. Getting close to the ground at high speed except for landing is generally frowned upon and can even be dangerous. But in tactical fighters, it is necessary to avoid enemy radar and antiaircraft guns that cannot be aimed to that low angle.

My student on this flight was an average pilot with whom I had not flown previously. The briefing, taxi, takeoff, and departure were all normal and procedurally correct. My job was to fly loose formation, keep track of the intended and actual courses we were flying, check our altitude, airspeed, and the time over each checkpoint so that I could grade the student fairly. We approached the low-level starting point and descended to our preplanned five hundred feet above the ground. The first leg went well. He maintained good airspeed and elevation while contouring the terrain. I began to think I had underestimated this student.

When we turned at the second checkpoint, I noticed some clouds ahead and wondered if they would be too low for us to continue the planned route. The student did not say anything and continued as he had done up to this point. As we progressed along the route, it became clear we would not be able to continue the flight in visual conditions. Rather than deciding to abort the low-level mission and stay out of the clouds, he flew right into them.

I immediately told him to get on instruments and start a gentle climb. I was now in close formation so I could keep him in sight and check my flight instruments to make sure we were climbing on a level course. I knew the next problem could be the student might get vertigo and become disoriented in the clouds. I told him to look to his right and see me. I was taking the lead and told him to fly close formation on me.

Our only recourse was to climb so there would be no danger of hitting a mountain and then return to clear weather. We did not have clearance to fly instrument flying rules (IFR), but that was not my immediate concern. I just wanted to keep the student pilot on my wing, get to a safe altitude, fly smooth instruments, and get out of the clouds. After a few minutes, we returned to visual flight and could see the ground and blue skies ahead. We aborted the lesson and flew back to the base and landed.

There were several lessons learned that day. The flight should have been cancelled before taking off because of the weather over the low-level route, but there had been no reports from any source about the weather conditions. The student should have made the decision to abort the route and stay in visual flight rules (VFR) conditions. I should have had him abort the route before entering clouds. The student personally experienced vertigo and witnessed the danger it can be, especially at low altitude. I complimented him for flying good formation in the clouds and called the experience an aborted flight. I did not grade him but did thoroughly debrief him on several items we experienced on the short flight. I think we both learned some valuable lessons that day and lived to fly another day.

MACH 2 TEST FLIGHT

Airplanes are complicated machines and must be thoroughly maintained to be safely operated. We had a very large fleet of F-104 aircraft at Luke AFB to support two squadrons of instructors and German Air Force (Luftwaffe) student pilots. We instructed new pilots who had never flown anything but a trainer. Our course was very advanced. The training included transition (learning to fly the aircraft), acrobatics, formation, instrument flying, weapons delivery in skip and dive bombing, rocket delivery, air-to-ground strafing, and air-to-air gunnery. When our students graduated, they were qualified as fighter pilots and returned to Germany to join F-104 fighter squadrons.

Not long after arriving at Luke AFB and becoming a fully qualified F-104 instructor, I was asked if I would like to add additional work to my normal schedule. It involved flying, so, of course, I said yes and was checked out as one of the four Functional Check Flight (FCF) pilots that tested airplanes after maintenance work such as engine changes, etc. Everything had to work to ensure the airplane could be safely flown by any F-104 pilot.

Everything possible had to be checked on a complete FCF flight. There were several pages printed on checklist-size cards. Each task was placed in logical order so that it could be tested in sequence within the time and fuel capacity for the flight. A full FCF took a very busy hour to complete.

The highlight of the test was to climb to thirty-five thousand feet northwest of Phoenix and turn south into a "supersonic corridor." When level at altitude and the airspeed stabilized at nine-tenths the speed of sound, the task was to advance the throttle to full afterburner, start the clock, and time the acceleration to Mach 2 (twice the speed of sound). That is over 1,450 miles per hour. When Mach 2 was reached, the clock was stopped, and the elapsed time was recorded. If it was much more than sixty seconds, we recommended that the engine be retuned for better acceleration.

Typically, at thirty-five thousand feet, the jet exhaust left a distinctive white condensation trail that could be seen for miles. Since the test was at this specific altitude, we had to obtain clearance for the speed run in controlled airspace from Phoenix Air Route Traffic Control Center (ARTCC). That is the agency that controls all aircraft above eighteen thousand feet within their responsible airspace. Toward the end of my Mach 2 run, I heard a radio transmission from someone calling Phoenix Center. I do not know if it was an airliner or a private aircraft, but the pilot had obviously seen my condensation trail and the speed at which I was making it. His call said something like, "Phoenix Center, what is making the contrail at my twelve o'clock position at a high rate of speed?" Phoenix Center radioed back to the inquiring pilot, "That is an F-104 Starfighter from Luke Air Force Base, at thirty-five thousand feet, flying at twice the speed of sound."

The response from the pilot is something that I have never forgotten. His last radio conversation with Phoenix Center that I heard was a simple response when he said, "Oh, it is fun to go fast, and not many pilots get to go supersonic, let alone twice the speed of sound. Aren't fighter pilots lucky?"

I enjoyed being an FCF pilot during my three years at Luke AFB. It was challenging, increased my knowledge greatly, gave me more flying time than just instructing fledgling pilots, and yielded the satisfaction that every airplane I cleared was totally operational and safe for my fellow pilots to fly.

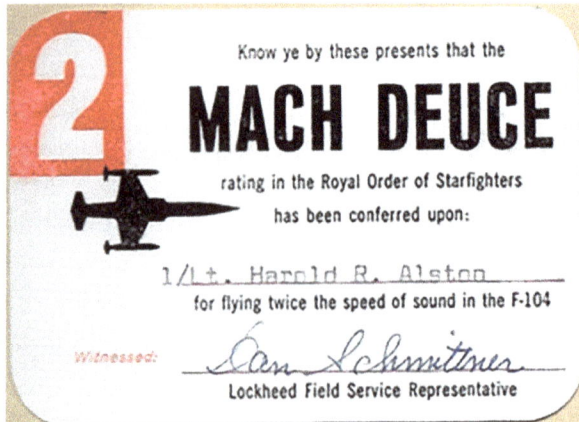

F-104 "Mach Deuce" card

TECH REP LOOP

Lockheed Aircraft Corporation manufactured the F-104 and provided in-house support at most locations where their airplanes were based. We always had a technical representative assigned to the four bases from which I flew the airplane. Those were George AFB, California, DaNang AB, South Vietnam, Udorn Royal Thai AB, Thailand, and Luke AFB, Arizona. They were worth their weight in gold because they knew the engineering and mechanics of the airplane in great detail and provided much help solving routine maintenance problems. They were also invaluable as unofficial members of accident investigation boards. The "Tech Reps" with whom I became acquainted were not only very knowledgeable but were outstanding men and became good friends.

A test flight involving a check on everything possible required a full hour, full fuel, and a very attentive pilot. There was a six-page checklist to follow just to accomplish everything.

Occasionally, a test flight was required for a specific problem. It could be the engine, radar, flight controls, etc. needing a thorough evaluation to confirm that the specific system or component was working the way it was designed before it could be released for daily scheduling. Such was the time one day when I was asked to test a two-seat F-104 that previously had trouble with wingtip flutter. Maintenance thought they had found and repaired the problem but still needed to confirm their work in the air at various airspeeds.

Since it was a two-seater, the Tech Rep asked me if he could go along on the flight. He was qualified and trained to ride in the back seat, had been trained on ejection procedures, intercom communications, and had his own helmet. I was happy to take him along, and it was to be an easy flight because it would not take very long to test the flutter. It would leave time and fuel to have some fun and let him fly the jet. That is always a big thrill for a non-pilot, especially for a Tech Rep who did not get to fly often. He could actually play with the airplane for its intended purpose rather than working on a dismantled aircraft on the ground.

The test went quickly, and I confirmed that I would release the aircraft for normal use. I gave control to the Tech Rep to fly while we still had plenty of fuel. We were at fifteen thousand feet cruising at four hundred knots (460 mph). Very smoothly, my passenger began to pull the nose up. I noticed he did not advance the throttle and was staying at one G. That was fine with me until we were at sixty degrees going for the moon. The airspeed was below 250 knots (287 mph) and decelerating slowly. Knowing we were in a steep climb, losing airspeed, and not knowing what his intentions were, I calmly asked: "What are you trying to do?" He responded, "Make a loop." Yikes!

I immediately said, "I've got it," and took the controls. I smoothly rolled to the right, inverted, and let the nose fall through the horizon. By then, we were at stall airspeed, and I did not want the airplane to go out of control in his untrained hands.

I applied power, returned to level flight, and instructed him that this airplane needs 500 knots (575 mph) at entry, full throttle, and four Gs to make a looping circle of 15,000 feet in diameter. We would have stalled and gone uncontrollable if I had let him continue. I proceeded to demonstrate a loop, talked about everything I was doing and what I was looking for at every critical point. I just considered my Tech Rep was one of my German students in the back seat and talked him through a safe loop. He was thrilled to fly a loop by himself, safely, with my coaching. He was really happy and proud to tell his friends that he actually flew a loop in an F-104G Starfighter. I am sure it made them jealous.

I was a very experienced instructor at the time and saved a lot of trouble by recognizing a potential problem, taking control of the situation, and later letting the Tech Rep accomplish his desire of flying a loop, but *why do I find myself in these situations?*

NO-FLAP LANDING

The F-104C Starfighter was built for speed. It had a powerful engine and small wings that were unique to this airplane. Each wing was only seven feet from fuselage to the outside tip. It was about two and a half inches thick and tapered to a sharp edge on the leading edge. It might be compared to a dull paring knife found in any home kitchen. I have seen pilots, not wearing flying gloves, accidentally bump their fingers against the leading edge and receive a minor cut drawing blood. What is worse is when a pilot squats on his haunches to inspect the landing gear and does not crouch quite low enough. The resulting penalty from gently bumping his head on the wing's leading edge causes a laceration on his hair-covered skull. No kidding, I have seen it happen. Since the wing is so thin, there are no fuel tanks, but honeycomb construction material covered with titanium for strength.

The airplane is so streamlined that there is very little drag. However, on the opposite side of the scale is that for the airplane to fly, it must be going fast enough to create sufficient lifting action. The same principle applies on approach to landing, meaning the airplane must fly fast to avoid running out of lift and stalling.

There are only three flap settings in the Starfighter. They are "up," "take off," and "land." There is no way to select anything in between those settings. I made hundreds of landings using flaps in the land position because that was the normal landing configuration. The normal flap position in the "land" position yielded thirty degrees down on the leading edge of the wing, forty-five degrees down on the trailing edge of the wing, and boundary layer air being blown over the trailing edge of the wing flaps. Final approach speed in this configuration is 175 knots (201 mph). I had also made several landings with the flaps in take-off position, especially when towing the dart air gunnery target. Landing with the dart rig mounted on the left wing required landing with flaps in the take-off position; otherwise, the left flap would strike the dart rig and damage would be the result. In that setting, the configuration is fifteen degrees of flaps on the leading edge of the wing with only thirty degrees on the trailing edge and no boundary layer air. The final approach speed in this configuration is 195 knots (224 mph).

Lockheed F-104 flaps (circled)

115

Now comes the "fun" part. I had never made a landing without flaps and was curious as to what it would be like to have that experience even though it was never practiced in training and was never necessary to land without flaps. I was just curious to see what the speed of approach would be like and to see how difficult it would be to stop the airplane on a ten-thousand-foot runway. With no flaps on landing, the approach speed had to be 225 knots (259 mph). That is fast and noticeably uncomfortable. The landing is all right, but trying to get the airplane stopped before running out of runway is the problem. I just had to try it once.

Because no-flap landings were not in the training syllabus, never practiced in tactical squadrons, and could burn out brakes just stopping the airplane on the runway, even with the use of the drag parachute, it was not something that needed to be done. Some might even consider it a dangerous event. If anything bad happened, the pilot would undoubtedly receive disciplinary punishment.

I was not going to make a practice no-flap landing at Luke AFB, which was our home base. Doing so without a valid reason, such as malfunctioning flaps, would probably be reported for stupid and unnecessary exposure to risk. I did not want to have to explain my reasons to the squadron commander or even higher…such as the wing commander. Because our primary job was training German pilots, there would never be an opportunity. However, I was an FCF pilot, and all the test flights were a single airplane with no wingman. If I worked fast on the test flight, I might have enough fuel to try my no-flap experience.

The next decision was to choose a runway. We had an emergency runway south of Gila Bend Arizona that was close to our gunnery ranges and within a few miles of Luke AFB. The Gila Bend runway was 8,500 feet in length, 150 feet wide at 826-foot elevation. Everything about Gila Bend was fine except for one thing. The runway was 1,500 feet shorter than Luke AFB. I began to question my intended folly. It would be difficult to stop in that distance so I decided I would make a touch and go landing. I would still experience the fast approach and touchdown speed and could get a feel for how much runway would be used before decelerating to 180 knots (207 mph) when the drag parachute could be deployed.

I found my opportunity and called the Gila Bend tower for an approach. They were very happy to oblige since they seldom had any traffic to break their monotony. I lined up to land from north to south and established configuration with the landing gear down and no flaps. I could easily discern the difference of speed on final approach compared to normal full flap landings…it was fast.

I touched down close to the end of the runway and kept the nose up to take advantage of aerodynamic braking. I was using up runway fast, so I lowered the nose slightly, pushed the throttle to maximum power, and took off with a couple of thousand feet of runway to spare. It was questionable if I could have stopped on the runway. Even with everything going perfectly, including the drag parachute opening fully, and using wheel brakes, without blowing a tire, it would have been close, if not impossible.

Returning to Luke AFB for my final landing of the memorable flight, I was happy to use full flaps, have ten thousand feet of runway, and know I could stop without any question and keep my secret. I never had the urge to make another no-flap landing in the six years of flying the F-104 Starfighter. Once was enough, and I never discussed it with anyone else. I may be the only fighter pilot I know to have intentionally made such a landing. Please don't tell anyone and help keep my folly a secret. *Okay?*

CHAPTER 11

★

US Air Force Academy, Colorado Springs, Colorado

A PUDDLE JUMPER OR A JET? DUH!

I received a call from Al Bache who was a very good friend and fellow F-104C pilot. He was serving as an Air Officer Commanding (AOC) of a cadet squadron at the Air Force Academy. He wanted me to consider coming to Colorado Springs, Colorado, to serve in the same capacity. He said it was a great stepping-stone for an important leadership position that would be an asset when considered for promotions and suggested that I pursue an assignment to the academy. I was a captain at the time and certainly wanted to be a major at my first opportunity. I asked if I would be able to maintain flying currency; after all, my career goal was to fly fast airplanes. Al said there were three ways to fly at the academy. First, I could instruct cadets in a T-41 Mescalero leading to a Federal Aviation Administration (FAA) private license. Second, I could be a sailplane (glider) instructor. Both options were flown from the academy airstrip on campus. The third option was to fly a T-33 jet trainer based at Peterson AFB, Colorado Springs.

I considered Al's invitation and respected his advice. Patsy and I discussed the potential opportunity. We did not see any disadvantages and thought it would be a great place to live with good opportunities for the boys to go to school and have excellent examples from the cadets. Plus, it would be a nice stable assignment for two to four years. I would be a commander, which I had never been, and it would be a great professional learning experience for me as a captain.

I informed the Military Personnel Center that I wanted to go to the academy. Al pulled some strings with the commandant's division, and I got the job. Usually, transfers like this were in the summer when school was out, but they wanted me there in January because the AOC of the 27th Squadron was being transferred, and the opening had to be filled as soon as possible. We were on our way right after New Year's Day.

It took all six of us plus a pet, Brittany spaniel, living in a two-bedroom apartment for three months before we were assigned a house on the academy campus. In the meantime, I processed in, was welcomed by the commandant of cadets (BG Robin Olds, a famous fighter pilot), found my squadron, met my cadets, and was officially an AOC. Now, for the rest of the story!

I was notified that I would be a T-41 instructor pilot teaching cadets how to fly an airplane. The T-41 was the air force version of Cessna 172 Skyhawk—a very basic airplane in which beginning students learned to fly. I had never flown anything that basic, and after flying a Mach 2 fighter, I did not want to fly a 140 mph "puddle jumper." The assignment was made by a colonel who was chief of the Cadet Military Training Division. He reported to BG Olds.

T-41 Mescalero

I did not know the commandant very well, but I did know the base commander, Colonel Jim Lannon. He previously had been the base commander of Luke AFB, Arizona, when I was an instructor there. He always came to watch tennis matches when I competed in base tournaments. I thought it would be a good idea to go see him, renew our acquaintance, and see if he had any pull with the colonel who had made my flying assignment.

I found the office of the base commander, told the secretary that I was an old friend, and asked if I could see him. She buzzed him on the intercom and told him I was there and asked if he had time to see me. With a smile on his face and hand outstretched to shake mine, he opened his office door and invited me in. We sat on sofas facing each other and reminisced about our Luke days. At an opportune time, I told him I had been assigned to fly the T-41 but was not happy about it. He asked what I wanted to fly. I told him I was a jet pilot all the way and preferred the T-33. After all, besides all my fighter time, I had a lot of T-33 experience as an instructor and flight examiner at TAC HQ at Langley AFB, Virginia.

To my surprise, he immediately went to his desk, picked up the phone, and punched a number. I only heard his side of the conversation, but it went something like this, "I have Captain Harold Alston in my office; he flew combat over North Vietnam, instructed German pilots in the F-104, and is the best fighter pilot in the air force, and I would like you to assign him to the T-33 instead of the T-41." After a few words back and forth, it was a done deal.

I promised Colonel Lannon that I would not let him down for making the change of assignment happen. Because of my experience, I was made the academy's T-33 instructor and flight examiner to give the required semiannual check flights that every active pilot must pass. I also led flybys for burials at the cemetery and supported Air Defense Command pilots based at Peterson AFB.

Sometimes, it pays to ask for what you want and not be satisfied with anything less. It worked for me at the academy. It was not the first time during my career that I asked for what I wanted. It was not the last time either.

CARRIER LANDING, YOU'VE GOT TO BE KIDDING!

As the academy's T-33 instructor/flight examiner, I flew with almost every pilot who was assigned to the T-33 for proficiency or to maintain requirements for receiving flight pay. One of those pilots was Major Ronald Fogleman. Ron was an instructor in the academy's Academics Department. We became friends when I certified him to fly formation. We occasionally were tasked to fly missing-man formations for ex-cadets or others who were being buried in the academy cemetery. I was usually the flight leader for those occasions. Ron was a very good pilot who had flown fighters, served a combat tour in Vietnam, and was an outstanding officer and example to the cadets.

On the commandant's side, where I worked as an AOC, we had a marine major serving an exchange assignment as an AOC. He was a graduate of the Naval Academy and was a Marine Corps jet pilot. Ron Fogleman was an associate AOC and worked occasionally with the marine's squadron. The marine major invited Ron to fly a cross-country flight to Navy Kingsville, Texas.

The major was going there to fly his quarterly currency requirements. Ron asked me if I would like to go with him. When I was told that we might be able to fly with the navy squadron while we were there, I jumped at the chance. It was a training base, and the navy fighters were the A-4 Skyhawk built by Douglas Aircraft Co.—the same type of aircraft that Senator John McCain was flying when he was shot down over North Vietnam.

Douglas A-4 Skyhawk

We flew from Colorado Springs, Colorado, to the navy base on a Friday. Our marine friend met us and took us to his squadron where we were introduced and made welcome. They had two two-seat A-4s ready to fly us in the back seat on a training mission. We were briefed on the cockpit items we needed to know, especially the ejection procedures, controls, switches, and etc.

We took off as a flight of two and flew to the range for the instructors to practice their work. I flew formation on the way. The airplane handled nicely, had a good feel, and responded smoothly to my control inputs. It was a better feel than our T-33. After the range work, the rest of the time was mine. I took the controls and immediately did an aileron roll. A few more rolls and several minutes of flying formation, both on the wing and as leader, and it was time to return to the base and land.

I flew the entry expecting that the navy pilot would take over and make the landing. The runway was painted like the deck of an aircraft carrier complete with stripes where the landing cables would be, and mounted on the left edge of the approach end of the runway was the famous Fresnel Lens Optical Landing System. More commonly, it was called the meatball, or simply the ball. Every aircraft carrier has one to insure a precise approach and landing. To my surprise, but to my pleasure, he instructed me to fly the aircraft all the way to landing. This was amazing. I would get to fly the Navy A-4 to a landing on a simulated aircraft carrier. I had made thousands of traffic patterns and landings in air force aircraft, so what would be so different this time?

The pitchout and landing pattern went well and was not much different than what I was used to. I turned onto the final approach with airspeed and descent right in the groove. As I rolled out on final approach, I saw the ball in the center of the screen exactly where it should be. However, as I progressed toward the runway, the ball slowly moved to the right indicating a correction was needed to keep it in the center. The only problem was that I had not been briefed how to fly the ball. I did not know which way to move the airplane to keep the ball in the center. Was it directional or nondirectional? In the short seconds trying to figure it out, the ball moved off the screen and disappeared; so much for flying the ball! I simply reverted to what I did know and continued the approach and landed the airplane. It was a good landing but a little long and would have caught the third or fourth cable on the simulated carrier deck.

My navy pilot congratulated me on a good flight and landing but said I had landed a little long and did not "fly the ball." I responded that I saw the ball move but did not know how to correct to keep it in the center. He laughed.

Back in the squadron, we hung our helmets and parachutes when the pilot I was with called the squadron to attention. He complimented both of us air force pilots for fine flights and then continued to describe my "carrier landing" and how I let the ball move off the screen and did not know how to correct my approach path to keep it visible. It gave the navy pilots a good laugh at me and the air force. Even with the embarrassment, the experience was worth every minute spent with our sister service.

I still do not know how to stabilize a moving ball. They would not tell me, and I guarantee you that I am not going to request an exchange tour with the navy just to find out. I am happy landing on runways and not a pitching aircraft carrier.

Postscript: It is interesting to note that Major Ron Fogleman, a graduate of the Air Force Academy, advanced through the ranks to

General (4 stars) and was appointed the fifteenth Chief of Staff—the highest position in the Air Force. He retired September 1, 1997.

CADET BAD WEATHER FLIGHT

One of the motivational experiences provided to cadets were flights in the T-33, two-seat jet aircraft. When the first year cadets, "Doolies," arrived, they were faced with discipline, rigid physical and mental training on the campus and in the field learning survival skills. To give them a break and to motivate them to be air force pilots and navigators, we gave them a half hour flight from Peterson AFB, Colorado Springs, Colorado, around Pike's Peak. For most cadets, it was the first time they had flown in an aircraft where they could pretend to be a pilot. We usually allowed the cadet to take the control stick and fly the aircraft. Some cadets were apprehensive; some were very eager, and a few got sick, but after landing, every cadet was excited to have flown a jet.

During the cadet's senior year as first classmen, they were offered a cross-country flight to a distant base where they would land, refuel, and then return to Colorado Springs. Usually, these cadets were already selected for air force pilot training following graduation. It is one of these flights that prompted the following.

One of the days that I was scheduled to fly a cadet on an out and back cross-country was a somewhat cloudy day. I planned to fly to Luke AFB, Arizona. I chose this for a couple of reasons. It was a comfortable distance to give the cadet a good ride. I had been stationed there and was very familiar with the area and the base. It was a fighter training base with F-100s and F-104s based there. What was better than a ramp full of fighters to motivate a future pilot?

Lockheed F-104Gs, Luke AFB, Arizona

The first leg of the flight was routine. The weather was good, and we got refueled quickly and were ready to return to Colorado Springs. We received a weather briefing for our return flight, and it forecasted worse weather than when we departed. The clouds were much lower, and it was raining, but there was no icing predicted. I was comfortable with the forecast to return and complete our round-robin flight.

Approaching Peterson AFB, we were given routine altitudes and navigation positions to make an instrument approach to the field. The minimum ceiling for the approach I planned to fly was two hundred feet above the ground and one-half mile visibility. That is low, but I was proficient in flying on instruments and was not concerned. During the flights, my cadet was very talkative, asked a lot of questions, and seemed very interested. As we intercepted the final approach course to Peterson AFB Runway 35 (landing to the north), I told the cadet that I did not want any talking from him as my total concentration was the approach, and I did not want anything to detract me from flying airspeed, course, glide path, and a safe landing.

I saw the end of the runway within one mile and no higher than two hundred feet. My final approach speed was 120 knots (138 mph). The landing was in solid rain, just as predicted, but I had no problem slowing the aircraft to turn off the runway and taxi to our parking spot.

I was surprised to see the base commander waiting for us as we walked into the operations building to hang up our parachutes. He had a smile on his face and said that he checked to see who was flying the airplane on the approach. He said he was at ease to see that it was me because he knew I was the academy instructor and check pilot and was probably the most proficient pilot flying in the cruddy weather. His concern was the handful of other pilots who were with cadets on similar flights and would be returning to Peterson AFB. He wanted my recommendation to either let them return with the low weather conditions or to hold them at their turnaround base until the weather improved.

I told him I had given annual check rides to some of them, knew their previous experience, and was confident they were proficient enough to land in the existing conditions. He took my suggestion and did not divert anyone to an alternate. They all returned safely and logged some great instrument time toward their annual requirements. "All's well that ends well."

WHY JUMP OUT OF A PERFECTLY GOOD AIRPLANE?

The title quotes a very common question among air force pilots. After all, they signed up to fly airplanes, not leave them while they are still in the air. Parachute jumping is a big deal in the US Army. Many soldiers are trained to be paratroopers. It is much respected for one to proudly wear the Parachutist Badge on his uniform.

The Air Force Academy was the only air force certified school to offer a parachuting course and award "Jump Wings" (parachutist badge). The army school only requires five parachute jumps to qualify, and they were all with a static line hooked to the inside of the aircraft so that it pulls the parachute open as the jumpers exit. The academy course required seven jumps. They were all free fall, meaning the jumper must pull the ripcord and open his parachute as he is falling through the air.

The course was established for volunteer cadets as part of military training offered at the academy. Parachuting was also offered to academy staff officers like me. Hooray!

During my first two years at the academy, I was AOC of the 27th Squadron. During the summer, I also commanded a Basic Cadet Training (BCT) squadron of one hundred new cadets. They reported in July to receive basic training before school started in September. It did not leave much discretionary time for anything else. My third year, I was elevated to executive to the commandant, so my summers were much more open. I always wanted to know what it was like to parachute, so I applied for the free fall parachute course.

I was accepted for testing to see if I was physically qualified for the rigorous training. It required tests every week for three successive weeks consisting of ten pull-ups, twenty-five sit-ups, twenty push-ups, and a one-and-a-half-mile run. We were only given thirty minutes to do everything…not much time to rest between events.

I was not concerned about any of the test except for the pull-ups. At the beginning of my training, I could not do more than five pull-ups. I trained every day on the monkey bars at the grade school. It was hard work, but I was able to complete the requirements within thirty minutes, and on my last test, I barely completed ten pull-ups. I was accepted for the next course scheduled to begin within a week.

There were only four other officers on the course. One of them was an army major who was already a qualified parachutist but wanted to free-fall jump. Since he already wore the parachute badge, this course was just for the fun of it. The rest of us had never parachuted before. Our instructor was a hard-core master sergeant, jumpmaster, with over 2,300 parachute jumps, including combat jumps in Vietnam.

We were taught in the classroom, practiced the proper way to leave the airplane, how to control safe gliding while falling through the air, when to open the parachute, and what to do if it did not fully inflate. We also learned operation of the reserve parachute, how to control descent to land at a particular spot, and how to execute a proper parachute landing fall to avoid injuries. We jumped off towers and did everything we could to replicate events that we would experience during a real jump.

Finally, we were ready to ride in an airplane and jump out of it. Our first four jumps were made with training parachutes that were thirty-five feet in diameter. We used twenty-eight-foot diameter parachutes, like the ones we used in fighters, for the final three jumps. The academy elevation is 7,200 feet. Six of our jumps were from ten thousand feet, about three thousand feet above the ground, free falling in a controlled "frog" position with our arms outstretched and legs spread. After a count of ten, we were instructed to pull the ripcord. In the instruction, I added my own silent prayer that the chute would open. As we climbed to altitude, the jumpmaster asked who wanted to go first. I immediately said "I do," which I also repeated on the next two jumps. However, after three jumps, he made me go last so he could chase me down.

I'll admit I had butterflies in my stomach as I stood in the open door of the airplane looking at the ground below before the jumpmaster tapped me on the shoulder and said, "Go."

Free fall parachute jump at the Air Force Academy

I established my controlled falling position and felt like I could fly without wings. It was very pleasant. After playing with aerodynamic maneuvering, I pulled the ripcord and put it in the pocket of my flying suit. When the parachute opened, I felt a pretty hard jerk and was glad my parachute straps were tight around my legs and chest. Looking up, I saw the beautiful circle of nylon lowering me toward the ground.

The descent was delightful. It seemed like suspended animation and offered time to look down on the drop zone and "miniature" houses, trees, cars, etc. in the distance. As I descended closer to the ground, I seemed to speed up. The ground was coming closer and faster than I expected. In my mind, I quickly rehearsed my parachute landing fall procedures and positions.

My landing was in the pea gravel drop zone. It was softer than I expected, and I was happy for such an easy contact with the ground with no injuries. I had successfully made my first "jump from a perfectly good airplane."

We jumped a couple of times a week which included one jump from fifteen thousand feet. This was interesting because it gave me more time to "body fly" and let the barometric sensor automatically open the parachute at ten thousand feet. There were three more jumps to make to complete the course. We were scheduled the following Saturday morning. I told my wife Patsy and suggested she consider bringing our four sons to the drop zone to watch me fall out of the sky. I made my three jumps (the maximum we, students, could make in one day) with all of the family watching.

Patsy and the boys pinned the Parachutist Badge on my flying suit, and we congratulated each of the other jumpers in the class and thanked our jumpmaster for his excellent instruction during the course. We all completed the training without injury or complications, and I had a new silver badge to wear on my uniform below my Command Pilot wings. I did not jump after that and, fortunately, never had to eject from my aircraft. The training and experience instilled total confidence and no fear of ejecting, if necessary, to save my life.

Postscript: I don't know if our sons were impressed by watching me parachute, but our oldest son, Douglas, also served a career in the air force in fighter aircraft. He earned his Parachutist Badge after training with the Marine Corps in Montana.

CHAPTER 12

★

Cold Lake, Alberta, Canada

LANDING AGAINST REGULATION

I had the distinct honor and pleasure to be chosen to attend the Canadian Forces Staff College in Toronto, Ontario, Canada. After my year there, my follow-on assignment was to the 434 TFS at Cold Lake Canadian Forces Base (CFB), Alberta, Canada. It was a long but fun road trip across the majority of Canada to get there, and I felt the anticipation.

Upon arrival, we were welcomed warmly by the squadron and the church members with whom we made instant friends. We were assigned a two-story house which was a good size for the six of us and was conveniently close to everything on the base including the squadron, the base hospital, exchange, commissary, officer's club, and tennis courts. The high school was off base in the adjoining town of Grand Centre, but the elementary school was only a short walk from our house.

The assigned aircraft for our squadron was the CF-5A Freedom Fighter, a two-engine, single-pilot fighter. In addition, we had ten of the same type aircraft but with a reconnaissance ("recce") nose configured with cameras instead of guns. I had never flown a fighter with two engines and had never even touched any model of the F-5. I looked forward to the new challenge and for a new fighter to be added to my credentials.

My first few flights were in a two-seat CF-5D with a squadron instructor pilot in the back seat. It did not take long to become acquainted with the cockpit layout, important airspeeds, and proper techniques to take off, fly, and land. I transitioned quickly into the single-seat CF-5A and was chased by my instructor in a separate aircraft. It was a fun transition, and soon, I was flying formation, tactical flights, and leading flights. I qualified in air-to-air refueling, strafe, dive bomb, skip bomb, instrument flying, and "recce" missions.

Major Harold Alston, CF-5A, 434 Squadron

At the time, I was a major in the USAF with hundreds of hours in fighters, two combat tours, a qualified instructor, flight examiner, and functional maintenance check pilot. When I became fully qualified in the CF-5A, they assigned me to be an assistant flight commander. I later became a flight commander and finally the squadron operations officer (second in command of the entire squadron).

Cold Lake is way up north in the province of Alberta. The temperature is very cold in the winter. We coped with rain, snow, fog, low clouds, and low visibilities. Our closest alternate airport was 180 miles to the southeast at Saskatoon, Saskatchewan, Canada. Cold Lake did have a very good GCA to direct us by radar on course and glide path to a safe landing. The minimums for the GCA approach were two hundred feet above the ground and one-mile forward visibility. If the pilot could not see the runway at this point, a go-around was necessary. That could lead to diverting to an alternate if there was enough fuel remaining to fly that far.

On the day in question, I was leading two wingmen. There were several other aircrafts flying that period also. Upon our return to Cold Lake, the weather had deteriorated significantly since we took off. It required us to fly a GCA to landing. Most of us would be returning about the same time and would have reduced fuel. That was not critical but was a consideration with no time or fuel to waste.

My flight was first to return, and we were established in the GCA pattern. I told my wingmen to maintain their positions with one on my left wing and one on my right wing. Written regulations only allowed a flight of two to make formation landings. However, sometimes, regulations do not cover every situation, and I decided this was one of those times. I had no doubt that I could make the landing on our first attempt, so I kept us together to give more time to the other less experienced pilots behind us to fly their approaches before the weather got worse.

The GCA controllers did an excellent job as we approached the runway on course and on the glide path. At a final approach speed of 140 knots (161 mph), I gave the signals to lower the landing gear and the flaps. I concentrated on my instruments. My wingmen concentrated on flying formation. Finally, I saw the runway over-run and runway lights. Within seconds, I landed on the centerline. Each wingman landed on their side of the two hundred-foot wide runway still in formation. I instructed number 3, on my right wing, to deploy his drag parachute and increase distance from me so he could control his own deceleration by the end of the runway. Three seconds later, I gave the same instruction to number 2 on my left wing. Each wingman's drag chute deployed normally, as did mine. Safely on the ground and with adequate spacing, each of us taxied off the runway, jettisoned our drag chutes, and parked in our assigned locations. Incidentally, every aircraft behind us had adequate time for their approaches and made safe landings before the weather closed in.

As I exited my aircraft, Major Chuck Sawchuck ran screaming to me that regulations clearly stated that only two aircraft in formation could land at the same time. I said, "I know." He yelled back, "Why did you do it?" I said I had confidence in my wingmen, and we needed to land quickly so that the other aircraft could land before the weather got worse. Any delay with either of my wingmen flying a separate GCA pattern would just waste time and could force someone else to divert to an alternate with low fuel. It was a prudent thing to do in my mind, and everything worked just as I had planned. Fortunately, after my explanation, Sawchuck never reported me for violating a regulation.

My theory is that regulations cannot cover every possibility when flying high-performance fighters. It was also not the last time I disregarded a regulation, but please do not spread that around.

FLAMEOUT IN THE DART PATTERN

In other assignments, I had flown many air-to-air gunnery missions for practice and qualification. To be fully qualified in every facet of weapons delivery in the CF-5, I was scheduled to fly as number 3 in a four-ship formation to shoot at the dart at Canadian Forces Base (CFB) Cold Lake. Unfortunately, it was in a two-seat trainer model that did not have guns in the nose. We also had a HQ staff fighter pilot, qualified in the CF-5, who was visiting our squadron. He was fully qualified in the airplane and was there to maintain currency, log some time, and evaluate several areas of our squadron. Being instructor qualified, he would evaluate my dart patterns and aircraft control. And if I met all the requirements, he would sign me off to shoot the guns in the fighter. While I had more experience shooting at a dart than any pilot in the squadron, I had to complete the requirements on their terms to be fully qualified. I did not mind because maybe I could demonstrate some techniques that could be of use to their pilots.

I previously noticed the second element of two aircrafts, with which I had flown, were good taking off in formation but were lousy in joining with the lead element. It was common to see them too far back requiring them to fly faster to join with the lead element. It took more fuel and time for the formation to get together.

On takeoff with my wingman, I saw a perfect opportunity to demonstrate how they should join with the leader and his wingman. It really is not that difficult. Number 3 (me in this case) just had to get inside the lead element's turn, closing distance, and sliding in position effortlessly much sooner than their normal dragged in join up.

My wingman stayed in excellent position as I negotiated the turn and closure. We slid under the lead element to our position on the right wing using half the time and fuel to accomplish the join up. The staff instructor in my back seat said, "That was a beautiful join up. I wish I could get our pilots to join up like that." That was a good start to my evaluation.

The first two aircraft each flew their dart patterns and took their live shots. I don't remember if they hit the target, but it was still very stable when I got my first chance. The pattern began about a thousand feet higher than the target while flying parallel to the target. We called it the perch. I was cleared by the dart tow pilot and began my attack. The procedure was to lower the nose, accelerate, and fly toward the dart. Halfway into the attack, the turn is reversed to reduce angles and to aim the guns on the dart.

I do not know why, but as I reversed my turn, the right engine flamed out. My staff pilot, in the back seat, said, "We have a flame-out." Duh! I already knew it and, immediately, was executing the restart emergency procedure. The engine started, and I advanced the throttle while I continued flying toward the dart for our simulated attack. My back seat pilot complimented me for restarting the engine so fast and still making a credible attack on the dart.

Needless to say, I had two demonstrations that I hoped would improve Canadian flying techniques. That was why I was there in the first place, and my check pilot certified me with positive remarks. Looking back, I was happy the engine started on the first try, or I would have had to abort the flight. I had flameouts later in my career but never again when I was attacking a dart or any other target. I guess it was just another square filled, but why me, and why in the middle of an air-to-air gunnery pass?

AFTERBURNER FIRE

Arnold Tombal was an exchange pilot from the Netherlands just like I was from the United States. We became good friends and flew together as often as we could. He also was my assistant flight commander. Arnold was married to Femke, a former speed skater. My wife Patsy brought her to Salt Lake City where they skied in our famous snow at Snowbird resort.

Simulated air-to-air combat flights were my favorites. The same was true for Arnold. This flight was to be one of those fun exercises. The mission was two CF-5s flown by squadron pilots against Arnold and me in our CF-5s. Since aircraft performance was identical, it boiled down to who were the best pilots that would win the aerial battle.

I led the flight of four with Arnold on my wing. We climbed to altitude where we split into flights of two and turned ninety degrees away from each other to obtain spacing. After a few miles, we turned back toward each other for the fight to begin.

Arnold was on my left wing, but because of the location of the two fighters that we were going to engage, we needed to be in echelon right (wingman on the right wing) so both of us could see the "enemy." Rather than take time to move Arnold to my other side, I radioed him to take the lead and commence the attack while I became the wingman.

Arnold responded quickly, so we did not lose any time positioning us for an attack. He immediately engaged both afterburners to gain more speed. I was about to engage mine and take spacing to fighting wing formation as a good wingman should do. Instead, I quickly broadcasted on the radio a quick call to Arnold to "come out of afterburner" and "knock it off" (disengage the fight).

Why, you ask? I had a good reason. As Arnold's afterburners lit, I observed a spot on the right fuselage that was rapidly getting dark from the paint burning. Arnold responded immediately, but by the time he came out of afterburner, a fire had burned clear through the fuselage. I relayed the message to Arnold. I knew immediately what had happened. An afterburner fuel spray bar had cracked, and the burning jet fuel was making a new pattern through the side of the airplane instead of out the back of the engine.

I instructed Arnold to head back to Cold Lake for a precautionary landing and told the other two aircraft to fight against each other to complete their mission. As we flew toward the base, Arnold did not want to take any additional chances with the right engine, so he shut it down and continued on with just the left engine.

I stayed in formation with a couple of wingspans between us. He flew a straight-in approach to a single-engine landing. When he safely touched down, I pulled away to make my own landing. Our mission was over. After I taxied to my parking spot, I walked to Arnold to have a close look at the damage. As we met, he threw his arms around me for saving his life. If the fire had burned longer, things could have gotten much worse. He said he did not want to end up ejecting from a burning airplane. He had already experienced escaping from an airplane over the North Sea and did not want a second ejection.

Maintenance discovered the problem that was what I suspected, replaced the nozzle, repaired the damage, and inspected both engines. Arnold was most thankful I had made the change in formation that put me in position to see the problem develop and take corrective action so quickly. Sometimes, we are lucky for reasons unknown. This was one of those times.

I just did my job as he would have done for me. It did not matter… Arnold insisted that he and Femke take Patsy and me to a nice restaurant dinner to express his gratitude. I thought it unnecessary, but we did have a very enjoyable social night out together without our children.

BOMB FUSE SETTINGS

Being an exchange pilot with a Canadian fighter squadron was a distinct privilege. I hope the Canadian pilot who was my reciprocal exchange pilot felt the same way while he served in a USAF squadron. I think the Canadians received a bigger benefit from us because of our better training and experience. For instance, they had not participated in actual combat since the Korean War in the early 1950s. The USAF had several years of combat action in Southeast Asia only a few years before I went to Cold Lake. My experience of two combat tours was an asset for teaching tactics and lessons learned from those experiences. Specifically, I dropped a lot of M117, 750 pound bombs on numerous targets in combat. My Canadian squadron dropped the same bombs once a year for practice. However, as I talked to pilots, they reported that many of the bombs hit the ground as duds. They did not know why.

In Vietnam, we dropped the bombs from a 30 degree dive angle, with computed depression setting on our gun site, at a specific airspeed of 450 knots (517 mph) and from a specified altitude of approximately 1,000 feet above the ground. Our fuses were set for two seconds. Those parameters gave us time to pull out of the dive and be safe of any danger from the exploding bomb.

I visited the supervisor of armament who had the responsibility of delivering, mounting, and setting the fuses on the airplanes. I asked him if he had a theory as to why there were so many duds. He responded that he knew exactly why the problem existed. He said because of Canadian regulation, he was required to set the fuses at four seconds. He also had tried diligently to get the regulation changed to prevent so many duds. Because of safety reasons, Canadian HQ was hesitant to make a change.

The squadron commander was going to be out of town one weekend. As squadron ops officer, I was in command of the squadron while he was gone. I thought this would be a good opportunity to test my solution to the bombing problem. I arranged to use the Canadian Army's live firing bombing range located a few miles south of our base. Scheduling produced aircraft to allow every pilot in the squadron to fly a mission delivering two live M117 bombs on the range. I told the armament supervisor to order and produce enough bombs for the exercise. In secret, I told him to arm the bomb fuses at two seconds; he was elated and smiled widely in total support. We told no one of our plan.

The pilots loved the exercise. They got to do something for which they were trained but with real bombs instead of the twenty-five-pound practice bombs they usually dropped. I met each aircraft when they landed to get their report. The pilots had big smiles on their faces when they reported it was fun seeing their bombs explode on the target.

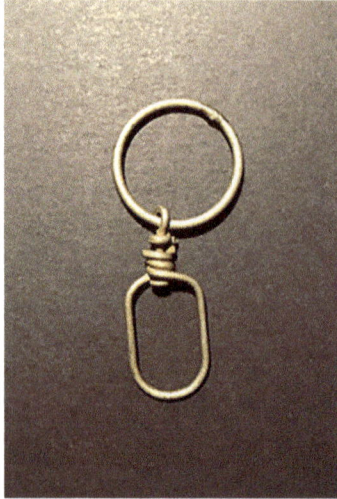

Bomb arming wire

As a result, I wrote a report to HQ describing the success of our exercise and requested that the regulation be rewritten stating the use of two second fuse settings to replace the current four second requirement. After coordination with the armament supervisor, he gave a hearty approval and said I had become his newest best friend for trying to get the restrictive and obsolete fuse setting changed.

With some concern for what I had done while the squadron commander was gone, I briefed him on the purpose and results of the exercise and immediately got his approval to send the request to HQ. I was worried about repercussions and what HQ might do to me for noncompliance of their regulation, but fortunately, they agreed with me and changed the regulation as I recommended. Whew, I dodged another bullet...or perhaps a bomb.

DOUBLE ENGINE FLAMEOUT

After major maintenance or for specific problems that have been repaired, it is usually required that airplanes be scheduled for an FCF to ensure that everything works as designed. It takes most of the fuel and at least an hour working as quickly and accurately as possible to get everything checked. I had previously had the privilege of being an FCF pilot at Langley AFB in the T-33 and at Luke AFB in the F-104G. This story is about an FCF at CFB Cold Lake.

On a rare day, when I was not scheduled to fly, I was working in my office when the telephone rang. It was the squadron maintenance supervisor. He said they had completed extensive inspections and minor tasks on a CF-5A and asked if I could fly the FCF so it could return to normal scheduling. Not wanting to be welded to my desk the rest of the day, I responded that I would love to.

Northrop CF-5A, 434 Squadron

As always, I made a detailed preflight inspection and found everything to be in order. The cockpit checks were also good. Engine start, taxi, takeoff, and climb were all normal. Our test area was several miles north of the base. There was a restricted area between the base and the test area, so I had to avoid it.

The several items to check on the climb were all in the green (normal). The most fun part of the FCF was at forty thousand feet. It was required to light both afterburners and accelerate to supersonic airspeed. My test run was west to east which took me farther away from the base, but it was not a problem because I had plenty of fuel.

I advanced both throttles into afterburner and expected to feel the thrill of acceleration from the extra thrust. Instead, I was completely surprised that instead of the afterburners lighting as they always had, this time, both engines flamed out resulting in absolutely no thrust. It was a surprise because I had never had this problem before. I had experienced flameouts but had always been able to restart the engine.

The engines in the CF-5A were a little different from others I had flown and could not be restarted above twenty-five thousand feet. Being eighty to one hundred miles away from CFB, I turned to glide directly to the base figuring I could arrive with enough altitude to make a dead stick landing if necessary. Dead stick landing is gliding to a landing with no power. It takes good judgment and maybe a little luck.

A direct flight would take me through the Aerospace Engineering Testing Establishment (AETE) restricted area. I called them on the radio for permission to enter their restricted area. They denied my request and said I would have to fly west and go around it. I informed them that I could not do that because of a double engine flameout, and if I could not make Cold Lake, I would have to eject, and the airplane would crash and be destroyed. I guess a light turned on in the controller's brain because he understood my emergency and cleared me directly to Cold Lake. If there was anything going on in the restricted airspace, he terminated it so I had priority.

There was nothing I could do except maintain best gliding airspeed and keep descending toward the base. It was the quietest ride I had ever had in a jet. As I descended below twenty-five feet, about halfway to Cold Lake, it was time to try restarts. First the left engine...it started, so at least I had single-engine power and would be able to get home even if the other engine did not start. I moved the air start switch for the right engine. Guess what? It restarted, and I was back to normal.

I continued to CFB and made a routine landing without any more worries. The aircraft had passed most of the FCF items except one, albeit an important requirement. I wrote the fault in the maintenance forms so they could adjust the engines, and I was happy to bring the aircraft back in one piece.

I telephoned AETE and thanked them for letting me bust through their sacred airspace that allowed me to bring the airplane home. They were happy that I made it home safely and that their accommodation was helpful. Thank you, guys.

JUST DON'T BREATHE

Captain Chuck Winegarden and I flew a couple of CF-5A aircraft from Cold Lake Canadian Air Base in Northern Alberta, Canada, to Trenton Air Base, Ontario in Eastern Canada. Trenton was the home base for the Canadian Boeing 707 aircraft that were configured as tankers. Unlike our USAF tankers that refueled one airplane at a time, the Canadian tankers could refuel two at a time from hoses on each wingtip.

After a weekend conducting some squadron business, we were scheduled to return to Cold Lake Sunday night. The plan was to fly with the tanker that was going to Cold Lake to be in position for our squadron to maintain qualification in air-to-air refueling. That was very convenient for Chuck and me because we would refuel a couple of times and would not require our landing in Manitoba, Canada, for fuel and take a couple of hours longer to get home.

After our preflight inspections, we were ready to begin our flight home. As we taxied out for takeoff, I noticed the ground crew had not filled my liquid oxygen system when we were refueled. The indicator showed about 25 percent remaining. I was in a dilemma for not catching it sooner. Shame on me! I rationalized that if I ran out of oxygen, I could descend, land at a Canadian air base, and make it home later than planned. Or, I thought, just keep flying and see if there is enough oxygen left to get me all the way to Cold Lake.

I decided to chance it and stay with Chuck and the tanker. My cross-check included the oxygen gauge every time I check my instruments. We made our final connection with the tanker and were within range of home, so we left the tanker and pushed up the power for a faster cruise. We began our slow descent but at a high speed about a hundred miles east of Cold Lake.

As we prepared to land at a lower altitude, I knew my oxygen system was still keeping me alive. I suffered no hypoxia symptoms and landed with almost no oxygen left. I was lucky and dodged a bullet. I made sure our maintenance crew refilled the liquid oxygen system and offered a silent prayer for having enough to breathe for the lengthy flight. After all, I was the reason for putting myself in that situation.

CHAPTER 13

★

Dhahran, Saudi Arabia

THE NEXT ASSIGNMENT

After my two great years flying with the Canadians, my next assignment was remote to Dhahran, Saudi Arabia, without my family, for twelve months to instruct Royal Saudi pilots in their new F-5Es. There were a few reasons I was not happy with this. First, I had been asked and encouraged to apply to lead the air force demonstration team—the Thunderbirds. My application had been accepted with several general officer recommendations, and I thought I had a good chance to be selected. There were two other applicants: Donnie Tribble, who I knew well and had flown with many times including combat missions, and Don Cherry, the other applicant who I did not know.

The first step of the Thunderbirds selection process was to ascertain if applicants were available, which Dan and Donnie were. To my surprise, I was not. I had orders for Saudi Arabia, and the assignment was under a contract between the Saudis and the US State Department. The State Department would not consider releasing me from the assignment, so I was disqualified to compete.

In preparation for the new assignment, I was required to attend a school at Eglin, AFB, Florida, to learn customs, what was socially acceptable as well as what could be offensive to their culture. When that was completed, I was sent to Williams AFB, Arizona, to check out in the new F-5E "Tiger Two." It was a different fighter from what I had flown in Canada—bigger, faster, had better equipment, and was a much more modern aircraft in general.

Saudi Arabian Northrop F-5E Tiger II

The transition into this new airplane was quite easy for me. The instructors were very well-qualified and knowledgeable, and with my experience, I had no trouble understanding the technical manual regarding the use of the new equipment. Emergency procedures were straightforward and easily memorized. The flying training was most enjoyable. Takeoffs and landings were easy to get used to and acrobatics, formation, and instruments were a piece of cake.

My final flight at Williams AFB was the required proficiency check flight. My examiner was a well-qualified captain who briefed me on what he wanted me to fly for him to evaluate. He flew close formation on my wing throughout the flight. The last maneuver, before returning to the base, was for me to fly a lazy eight. If you drew what the maneuver looks like, it would be in the shape of the number 8 lying horizontally on its side. What makes this maneuver difficult is that airspeed, pitch, and bank are very precise and are continually changing throughout the entire maneuver.

In a previous story, I explained how I learned to improve my lazy eight technique by singing "Up a Lazy River" to myself. It helped then, and it helped me on my check ride. In the debriefing and written on my final evaluation, the instructor commented that my lazy eight was perfect in pitch, bank, and airspeeds—something he had never observed in all previous check rides that he had evaluated. It was obvious that I passed the evaluation and was finished with the course.

Thank you, Lieutenant Prophet, for instilling a technique that stuck with me for twenty years of flying. I thoroughly enjoyed my time flying at Williams AFB and was very happy to arrive in Saudi Arabia fully qualified in their new airplanes.

Postscript: Don Cherry was selected as the commander/leader of the Thunderbirds and did an excellent job.

BAD START AT DHAHRAN

After attending the school to learn how not to insult Arabs and checking out in the new airplane, I had a few days with the family. Patsy and the boys wanted to spend the year without me in Salt Lake City, Utah, where we had families. They also wanted to ski in Utah snow which is world-renown. We bought a house in a nice neighborhood that was convenient to schools, church, and shopping. I had enough time to get our household goods and family settled before I began my commercial flights to the other side of the world.

Arabs in their thobes, gutras, and agols (everyday dress for Arab men) was a totally new sight for me. Few spoke English, and time and efficiency meant nothing to them. Fortunately, USAF people met me at the airport after I checked through customs. It was a totally new kind of experience for me until I was settled in my room in a modern barracks right on the Dhahran Airport. Commercial aviation was on one side of the airport, and the Royal Saudi Air Force was on the other side. We even had our own runway.

Major Harold Alston in Dhahran

There were six of us American pilots in our group that were sent to train new pilots in the F-5E Tiger II fighter. Normally, I would have begun flying within a couple of days, but unfortunately, my hold baggage (flying equipment, etc. that had shipped separately) had not arrived and would not be delivered for a week or two.

Rather than have me cool my heels doing nothing, I was sent to London, England, to attend the Farnborough Air Show and observe what the Saudi visitors were interested in. That was not a bad deal as Farnborough was the biggest air show in the world. I found a hotel room near Trafalgar Square in London. It was fun for me to be a tourist and see almost everything London had to offer. I still took the train to the air show three of the days I was there. It was a great vacation.

Returning to Dhahran after a week of leisure, I found my shipment had arrived so I could begin flying. I had met my other five American colleagues, so I spent my first day meeting the Arab pilots and getting familiar with the squadron building and flight line. It was a nice facility, and the airplanes were within walking distance. The squadron was commanded by Saudi pilots: first by Prince Mugren followed by Prince Bandar, both members of the royal family. All the pilots and students spoke English fluently, so there was no problem with the language.

I was finally scheduled for my first flight on the second day back from England to be indoctrination to the local area and make landings to renew currency in the F-5F. I flew the front seat with another instructor in the back seat to show me landmarks. I had not forgotten any aircraft procedures, felt quite at home, and was happy to get in the air.

Saudi Arabian Northrop F-5F Tiger II

On takeoff, I was concerned that the visibility was not very good. There were no clouds that I could see, but I could not see much beyond the end of the runway. I asked my new friend in the back seat if we needed an instrument clearance. He answered no and that this was just a sandstorm (shamal) passing through, and it was usually no big deal. If he were not concerned, I wasn't either; besides, the sand going through the engine would polish the compressor blades.

I did not see much of the ground as we climbed and finally flew into blue skies at twenty thousand feet. Wow, that was a big shamal kicking up a lot of sand. I did not see much to orient me with the Arabian Gulf or the oil field fires around the city of Hofuf which were great landmarks for our local flying area. It was fun to pull a few Gs and fly several acrobatic maneuvers before landing. The flying weather had to improve after my first flight, or it would be a very long year.

During my year, there were only two shamals that rolled across the desert. They can be pretty nasty with very low visibilities and high winds.

Postscript: By the way, Patsy made a good choice to spend the year in Salt Lake City. Her father passed away while she was there and conveniently his funeral was when I was in Salt Lake City on a month's leave all the way from Saudi Arabia. However, skiing and the famous Utah snow were below expectations that winter, but the boys adjusted well and enjoyed the year anyhow.

Postscript 2: Prince Bandar Sultan later became the Saudi Ambassador to the United States for several years.

FORMATION REJOIN

The program at Dhahran, Saudi Arabia, was advanced training for new pilots who had been taught to fly by British instructors. Our job was to make them qualified fighter pilots in the F-5E Tiger II aircraft. The training was a building-block approach of learning basic tasks before progressing to more advanced tasks. The first phase of training was to learn to takeoff, fly in good weather, practice acrobatics, and learn to land. This was done in a two-seat F-5F with an instructor in the back seat.

Once accomplished to safe standards, the instructor and student switched places. This was the instrument phase with the student learning to fly the airplane safely without outside references. There was a hood in the back cockpit that could be pulled forward to shut out all visibility to the outside world and require only instruments to fly safely. It simulated flying in bad weather or even at night where there are no references to maintain safe orientation.

With the basics over, next came the real fun of learning to use the airplane in the way it was intended. Fighters usually fly in flights of two or four aircrafts depending on the requirements of the mission. Therefore, the next phase was to become proficient in flying in close formation. I love formation flying, and it was my easiest phase when I was in pilot training. It requires constant concentration because a small mistake could result in a midair collision. The basic position is with the wingman slightly lower than his leader, a few degrees, maybe thirty degrees back, and the wingtips separated by a few inches. Every fighter has something that can be used as a reference to maintain position; it could be the navigation light on the wingtip lined up with the leader's helmet or some other combination. The leader must be smooth while maneuvering so his wingman can follow and maintain the correct position. It is even more important when leading a formation with one airplane on one side and two on the other side. A close formation of four airplanes is routine.

One thing that must be learned is how to rejoin the formation back together after being separated. To begin the rejoin exercise, the leader makes a steep turn away from the wingmen. Each wingman would wait five seconds by counting "one thousand one, one thousand two, one thousand three, etc." The interval created sufficient distance after a 180 degree turn to place each aircraft in line behind the leader several hundred feet between each airplane.

In this exercise, and as the flight leader, I maintained the gentle turn and constant airspeed so each wingman could accelerate a few knots and turn inside of me to reduce the distance and time to return to my wing in close formation. Number 2 was doing a good job and had no trouble returning to my left wing in close formation. The trouble began when number 3 reported he had lost sight of me. I was astounded how two pilots (one was even an instructor) in the same airplane could not keep me in sight within a mile or two. I had no trouble seeing them, and I even had a visual on number 4 who was behind number 3. I gave them hints and practically flew their airplane to get them inside the turn until they visually located me again and could continue on their own.

We practiced rejoins several times after that first disaster. I guess my three wingmen sensed my disgust with my "sightless" number 3 on the first try that they would not dare repeat the same problem again. I have wondered if eyesight is reduced from living in a godforsaken desert that is frequently blowing sand in their eyes. I was happy to get them through that lesson and hoped the students learned something from it and that the instructor in number 3 got his act together.

NIGHT "JOIN UP"

I must begin this story by saying that during the time of my seventeen years of flying fighter aircraft, delivering all kinds of ordnance for training and in combat, I had never flown night ordnance deliveries. Frankly, I had no desire to thrust myself at the ground at 400 knots (460 mph) to hit a target with a bomb and pull out at a thousand feet above the ground with four or five Gs pressing me into the ejection seat in the dark of night. I like to see my surroundings, especially when I am close to the ground. At night, I am not fond of being close to the ground until I see runway lights in front of me.

With three months before I was to leave Saudi Arabia for a new assignment, I was asked to establish a night bombing range. We had plenty of real estate at our air-to-ground range that we routinely used in our weapons delivery training in daylight.

There was no electric power available at the range. The solution for some illumination on the ground was to have containers that I could fill with sand saturated with jet fuel and hope it would burn long enough for a flight to complete their practice. I coordinated with our maintenance people who offered to cut fifty-five gallon steel drums in half. Problem solved, I got a fuel truck and driver, a pickup truck for me, a couple of helpers with shovels, a measuring tape, and some butane lighters, and drove to the range.

We set up a disposable aiming point in the center of our illuminated barrels, complete with sand and jet fuel, symmetrically placed around the perimeter. It was rustic but served the purpose.

We did have one modern touch for the range. In addition to the burning barrels on the ground, we had the capability of launching illumination flares. This was accomplished by a separate F-5E keeping the range illuminated while the fighters dropped their practice bombs. The flares had a small parachute which delayed the descent long enough for the fighters to make their passes. There were enough flares to light the range for the fighter flight to deliver all the practice bombs. The flare aircraft did not participate in ordnance delivery. To de-conflict, the extra airplane flew at a slightly higher altitude and to the side of the ground target. It remained clear of the fighter's delivery patterns so there would be no danger of hitting a flare but still have sufficient illumination.

I was on site the first night we used the range, and all went well. The second night, I was the lead instructor with two students on my wing. It was the first for each of us to bomb at night. I briefed the flight on everything we would do from takeoff to landing. The flare ship pilot was Prince Mugrin, the squadron commander. I briefed that the fighters would take off first and fly close formation to the range. The flare ship would follow us to the range and set up his own pattern to drop the first flare.

All was progressing well until I saw that Mugrin was flying toward us as if to join with my formation. The closer he got, I could observe that he was too fast to join on my left wing. I could not take my eyes off him. As he approached, he realized he was too fast and banked hard left with about sixty degrees of bank. In that position, he lost sight of me. Finally, I gave up on him and pulled up to avoid a midair collision. He passed through our flight path and ended up on the right side of my formation. That was it for me, and I told him to proceed to the range on his own.

I did not want him flying formation with me and my two students. I kept my wingmen with me, and we landed normally. I was quite angry for the poor airmanship shown by the prince. It took me a few minutes to settle my angry nerves. My detachment commander saw I was upset and wanted to know what it was all about. I explained what went on and that we had avoided a midair collision. He prevented me from even talking to Mugrin so I did not include him in the debriefing. The reason to exclude him was so a member of the royal family would not lose face. I never had to fly night weapons delivery after I left Saudi. I left them with a night range, introduction to the night mission, and no answer to the question of, *Why do I find myself in these situations?*

Postscript: That was the last time I flew with Prince Mugrin as he was transferred to a government job. As I pondered the flight many times in the succeeding days, I counted my blessings for being vigilant, having had good wingmen, and the safe results of the incident that could have wiped out every one of us.

EJECT OR LAND

Air Force fighter aircraft are well-made, are kept in almost perfect flying condition, and are safe to operate. That being said, infrequently, something goes wrong. A part fails, weather conditions are unsuitable for flying, or a pilot causes a problem from which he cannot recover. Minor malfunctions are handled routinely, safe landings are accomplished, and the airplane is returned to maintenance experts to fix the problem.

As good as airplanes are, occasionally, something happens that results in decisions that must be made in the best interest of the crew regardless of what happens to the expensive aircraft. Such is this description regarding a new airplane and the two pilots who were flying it.

I was monitoring the flying schedule in the operations room at Dhahran, Saudi Arabia. The detachment commander and the fire chief hustled into the room and announced we had a two-seat F-5F airborne with a problem. The pilot in the front seat was a Saudi student, and in my opinion, the best Saudi instructor pilot sat in the back seat. On takeoff, the left main landing gear did not retract. Another aircraft visually inspected it and reported that it was turned about forty-five degrees to the left rather than straight with the longitudinal axis. Obviously, a component had failed to keep it aligned properly.

Our detachment commander was a lieutenant colonel who had been a navigator and later received his pilot wings. He had less pilot time than I had, so they wanted my opinion. I was the assistant detachment commander and was a major but had been selected for lieutenant colonel.

The conflict was that the fire chief needed time to foam the runway if the airplane were to make an emergency landing. Our boss said that the flight manual stated that in this situation, the pilots should eject, parachute to a safe landing, and let the airplane crash. I immediately recommended to the fire chief to foam the runway, tell the pilots to land in the foam, use the drag parachute immediately on touchdown, and use the right brake sparingly to keep the aircraft as straight in the foam as possible. Another experienced pilot on our team agreed with me, but our boss stuck to his guns about ejecting from the airplane.

I did not tell them that I had seen a similar emergency at Da Nang, South Vietnam, with a Navy A-4. It was a successful landing. I repeated what I recommended and described what I thought would happen. I told them to tell the instructor to land the aircraft in the foam as close to the end as he could, deploy the drag chute, use the brake on the right sparingly, and no brake on the left. I said that as the airplane slowed down, it would caster to the left and to not fight the turn. By then, they should almost be stopped or at least very slow.

We finally convinced our boss, and the fire chief gave the order to foam the runway from his handheld radio and word was passed to the pilots. The boss left with the chief to go to the runway and watch the landing. I wanted to go but was not invited. Our boss was angry at me for countermanding his decision.

The landing was accomplished; the F-5F stopped in the foam and had turned about thirty degrees left at the stopping point…just as I predicted. The airplane was saved; the pilots were safe and only suffered from a little foam on their boots as they walked away. The boss never said a word about the incident to me but seemed to hold a grudge for my disagreeing with his position. I seemed to always be walking on eggshells in our relationship from then on. I was glad for the outcome and was happier when my year was completed, and I returned back to the United States and a new job.

FLYING IN A SHAMAL

As I wrote earlier, my first flight in Saudi Arabia was in a shamal. This time, it happened again but was near the end of my year flying with the Royal Saudi Air Force. I was to fly as the instructor in the front seat with another member of our team, who was also a qualified instructor, in the back seat to fly an instrument practice mission. This was great because we rarely flew with another American member of our Technical Assistance Field Team. We did not brief one hour before the flight like we always did with students, but on the way to the airplane, we discussed what we would do on the flight. If we wanted to change anything, it would be done on the intercom between our two cockpits.

We were the only instructors flying that morning, but there were five or six Saudi student pilots who were flying other solo missions at the same time. My friend in the back seat was flying with the instrument training hood so he could not see outside but had to rely on the instruments in his cockpit. I put him in unusual attitudes from which he had to recover and return us to straight and level flight. I had him do a few acrobatic maneuvers without looking outside. He thought it was fun.

I kept looking to the west at what looked like deteriorating visibility. I suggested he push the hood back and have a look. We agreed that it looked like a shamal was heading for the area where the airport was located. I was not concerned about our being able to land from a radar approach since we were professionals and were used to landing in bad weather with low visibilities. My concern was for the Saudi students who were qualified in instrument flying but not as experienced as we were. I called our squadron operations desk and asked how many students were still in the air. When my answer was five, I suggested they recalled them all home while they could still fly a GCA before the visibility reduced below their capabilities. Since they had been watching the storm approach, they agreed with my suggestion.

We began flying all around our practice area to make sure each aircraft was returning toward the airport. It requires some spacing to control one aircraft at a time for a GCA. After a few minutes, everyone was under radar control and lined up individually for their approach to the runway. Our work was done herding sheep, and we called for our approach. Since it was a practice instrument flight, I told my pilot in the back seat to fly the GCA, and I would look through the shamal for the runway as we got closer. Being the professional fighter pilot that he was, he did an excellent job, and we saw the runway at about one-half mile; that was at minimum visibility for a GCA.

Every flyer that morning was safely on the ground as the storm got worse. Since we were finished for the day, I changed clothes and drove downtown. In the car, my visibility was so bad that I could only see one light post ahead of me. I don't know the standard distance, but it was measured in feet. I was happy everyone was safe, and it was the last shamal I experienced. I was also proud of the Saudi student pilots who did a good job with their instrument flying in actual conditions.

LANDING ON THE DESERT

At Dhahran Saudi Arabia, we ate most of our meals at a club located in our compound that served all the United States military stationed there. We, six fighter pilots, were only a small part of the military assistance team assigned there. We were usually the only ones who had breakfast there, but the evening meal brought in all kinds of people, both military and civilian. As a result, I met the Arabian American Oil Company (ARAMCO) chief pilot. ARAMCO was the big oil company that was mining millions of barrels from the ground and shipping them all over the world to be refined. The pilot's job was to support exploration teams everywhere in the kingdom.

I asked the chief pilot if I could fly with him one day when he was resupplying one of the exploration teams. He was happy to say yes, and he would be even happier to have another pilot along for the ride. The aircraft he flew was a Fokker F-27. It was built by the Dutch with over five hundred original models. It was used by several feeder airlines in the US. Even my wife flew on an F-27 from our home in Apple Valley, California, to Salt Lake City, Utah, and back with our newborn son. It cruised at 260 knots (299 mph), powered by two turboprop engines, was built to carry forty-four passengers, and had a range of 1,500 miles. Most of the ARAMCO seats were removed from the cabin so bulky cargo could be loaded for delivery to the exploration teams.

Fokker F-27 Friendship

On our scheduled day, I met my friend at the airplane. He told me the mission was to deliver supplies to a team located somewhere camped on the Empty Quarter (Rub' al Khali). This area comprised the southern third of the Arabian Peninsula. It was very large with not much there except sand and an occasional camel train of Bedouins. He instructed me to sit in the copilot seat so I would have a great view, and we could converse with each other.

We flew for about forty-five minutes directly to where the camp was. After seeing nothing but sandy desert, I could see some equipment, trailers, etc., and knew we were at our destination. I did not say anything but was curious about landing in the sand. I was more at ease when I discerned a "runway" on our final approach. The sand was hard enough that we did not have any trouble landing or taxiing to a parking spot close to the camp.

While the airplane was being unloaded, we had lunch with the team leader who was an Australian hired by the Saudis. He was very friendly to me and explained what they were doing and how they did it. He gave me a tour of the camp, the equipment, and explained processes used to discover oil. Most interesting was the portable plant that took brackish water out of the desert and processed it into potable water to drink. The yield was only 50 percent of the input.

Too soon, we had to leave our hosts and fly back to Dhahran. Our conversation was nonstop all the way home. It was a wonderful experience for me. I got to see things I never would have experienced before and never have since. My pilot buddies were extremely jealous that during the year that each of us served on the desert, I was the only one who experienced landing on it. Carpe Diem! (Seize the day!)

CHAPTER 14

★

Las Vegas, Nevada

A DREAM COME TRUE

After tolerating a year in Saudi Arabia, I was ready for a new assignment back in the good old United States. Before I received orders, I was given a heads-up from my major general brother-in-law who just happened to be the assistant director of Air Force Personnel Directorate. He said I was being considered for an assignment to Williams AFB, Arizona, and wanted to know how I felt about it. It was a very good assignment, but it was the same training squadron I had trained in the F-5E before going to Saudi. I said it was good, but my real desire was to go to Nellis AFB, Nevada, "Home of the Fighter Pilot." It was where the Fighter Weapons Schools were located and two squadrons of Aggressors. It was the heart of the best fighter pilots in the air force. The general understood my desire because he had been stationed there when he was a fighter pilot.

When I received my orders, before I left Saudi, I could not have been happier. I was going to Nellis AFB, to the 65th Fighter Weapons Squadron, Aggressors. I had already been selected to be promoted to lieutenant colonel, so that meant I would be the operations officer (second in command of the squadron.) with anticipation of becoming the commander.

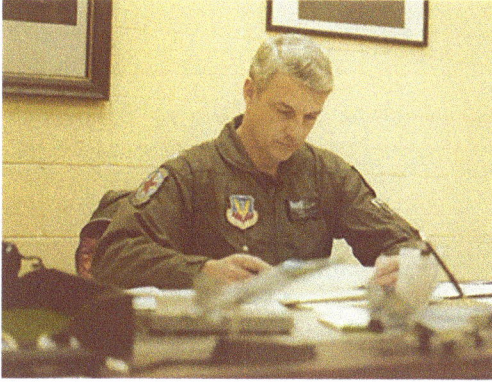

Lieutenant Colonel Harold Alston, Commander, 65th FWS "Aggressors"

Studies of the Korean War showed that our USAF fighter pilots achieved a ratio of fourteen and a half enemy MiGs shot down for every one of our friendly fighters shot down by MiGs. A similar study of the Vietnam War showed that our destruction of enemy aircraft ratio had dropped to about three (or less) MiGs destroyed for each US aircraft; that was a very poor ratio for current fighter pilots compared to previous experience.

There was a very good reason for the low-kill ratio for the US Air Force. It was a time when commanders were too "jinky" about accidents which usually got a commander fired. We could not train against unlike aircraft which resulted in a lack of knowledge, of performance, capabilities, and experience level in different types of airplanes. Training was restricted to only like aircraft within the same wing. That was finally changed when General Wilbur Creach became commander of Tactical Air Command, but it was too late for the Vietnam War.

The fundamental mission of the Aggressors was to train our friendly forces to become knowledgeable of potential enemy pilots and to become proficient in fighting against dissimilar aircraft. The aircraft we flew was the F-5E which simulated an MiG-21 in comparable size and performance. Aggressors flew formations and tactics that had been gleaned from classified documents of our potential enemies. The purpose was for our friendly pilots to learn to counter potential enemy tactics and thus improve the knowledge and capability to win rather than lose if they encountered the situation.

Mig-21 Fishbed and F-5E Aggressor

Aggressors were excellent fighter pilots who had been hand-picked from wings all over the air force. They were required to successfully complete comprehensive ground school and an even more demanding flying training course to become fully qualified as Aggressors who would fly against almost every aircraft type in the air force, navy, and friendly foreign country air forces.

The training took several weeks and began with the basics of flying a new model airplane for most pilots. I skipped that part because I was already qualified in the F-5E, so I began with one versus one in basic air combat maneuvering. I was experienced in these exercises and quickly breezed through to the next step. It was two versus two. That also was not new to me. Four versus four was always fun because it was difficult to keep track of who was a friend and who was an adversary.

I enjoyed the mission: deploying to other bases to fly with other aircraft, including Canada and all over the United States. I became a better fighter pilot even with all the experience from the past. Most of all, after only a few months, I became the commander of the squadron for the next two years. It certainly was a dream that came true.

DON'T FORGET ME

I don't remember why, but for some reason, I was flying by myself on one of our rare bad weather days at Nellis AFB. There was nothing to write about until I returned to land. Because of the low weather ceiling, it would require a GCA. A GCA required obtaining clearance from Approach Control and for them to identify me on their radar before we could commence the recovery for an approach. That being done, I was turned over to the GCA radar controller who would give me specific altitude and heading instructions all the way to landing.

I have flown many GCAs in my career and always had very professional service which brought me to a safe landing in all kinds of weather and low visibility. I had full faith in the Nellis controller to get me on the ground just like everyone else had previously.

I was given a vector to fly parallel to the runway that would take me north of the runway before making the turn to final approach. I followed his instructions. The controllers always communicated on the radio about every thirty seconds to give additional instructions, update the weather, or just so the pilot was comfortable that they were still following progress on their radar.

I do not know precisely how long it had been since I had heard from the controller, but my impression was that it had been too long. Maybe my radio had failed or his. I pushed the radio transmit button and said, "Nellis GCA, this is Sheik [my call sign]. Do you still have me on radar?" Immediately and in what I discerned as a panicked voice, he responded, "Turn right thirty degrees." I made the turn in great haste and rolled out on the new heading.

Just as I thought, he had been distracted and had momentarily forgotten me. Normally, it would not have been a big deal in open terrain. My problem was that I knew there were mountains northwest of Nellis, and I did not know how close the GCA pattern was to the mountains. I had been heading straight for them and would have flown right in to one on the heading I was flying. Hence, the panicked controller would have been responsible for my sudden death and the loss of an airplane if I had hit the mountain at 300 knots (345 mph).

My mental concern, probably a provident suggestion, and the quick instruction from the GCA controller to change direction saved my life. I survived the incident and lived to fly another day.

Why do I find myself in these situations?

"D," ALL OF THE ABOVE

As the squadron commander, it was infrequent that I was not the flight leader on most flights. My second-in-command was an experienced pilot and was the ops officer of our squadron. I told the scheduler to let Tree (his personal call sign) lead, and I would fly his wing. It would be the first time we had flown together, and I looked forward to the mission.

The briefing concluded, and it was time to get parachutes, helmets, and walk to our assigned aircraft. I accomplished my usual thorough preflight inspection and climbed into the cockpit where I checked that all switches and controls were properly set. Engine start was normal; Tree received clearance, and we taxied to the end of the runway, in formation order, for a final exterior aircraft check by qualified maintenance personnel. We all checked out and returned our salutes to the maintenance team.

We received clearance to taxi onto the runway and were cleared for takeoff. We extended the nose strut, throttled the engines to full power for a final check, and I signaled to Tree that I was ready. After checking the two wingmen on the right side for their response, Tree put his helmet against the ejection seat headrest and tipped his head forward. That was the signal to release brakes, begin our formation takeoff, light the afterburners, and smoothly accelerate and lift into the air free from contact with the concrete runway.

It sounds routine so far, doesn't it? Everything was as normal as formation takeoff should be. We retracted the landing gear, came out of afterburner, and the other two aircraft joined in close formation on Tree's right wing. I glanced at the landing gear indicators to make sure the wheels were up and locked. The indicators did not present the normal "up" position.

I immediately transmitted my malfunction to Tree and pulled up to keep my airspeed from accelerating. I lowered the landing gear lever, and the wheels came down and locked. After two or three attempts to retract the landing gear to "up and locked" indication and with Tree inspecting, we determined the gear was not going to fold into the wings properly and allow the covering doors to close.

My only recourse was to abort the mission and return to the base. I left the landing gear down and locked. As I turned to leave the formation, a generator failed and illuminated the warning light. Now I had two problems and things were getting worse. Fortunately, I was not very far from Nellis AFB and just wanted to get the airplane on the ground as soon as possible.

Northrop F-5E Aggressor with gear down

I notified the control tower that I was returning to Nellis AFB with malfunctions. They approved the return and asked the nature of my problems in case they needed to scramble the crash trucks as a precaution. I relayed my landing gear problem, generator failure, and a couple of other minor concerns when Tree transmitted in a cool, relaxed voice, "D, all of the above."

We all got a chuckle about Tree's description of my malfunctions as if it were a multiple-choice exam answer. He and his two remaining wingmen continued on their assigned mission, and I landed without further problems. Some days are like that but, gratefully, not too often. It was all in a day's work but disappointing.

LAST AIR FORCE FLIGHT

It has been said that all good things must come to an end. My air force career was no exception. Being commander of the 65th Aggressor Squadron was a dream come true for a fighter pilot. I had done a good job and had wonderful flying experiences, but my two-year term as commander was coming to an end. Nothing lasts forever.

I wondered what the AF had in store for me. I had been selected to attend the highest military postgraduate school which was an advantage for advancement. I had completed Squadron Officer School as a captain; I completed the Canadian Forces Staff College in residency as a major, and I had completed the Air Command and Staff College by correspondence. Now there were several alternatives such as Air War College, Army or Navy War Colleges, or the Industrial College of the Armed Forces (ICAF). I had already graduated from ICAF through correspondence. I had the diploma and did not want to attend another year of school. I was also tired of moving. That excitement had been fulfilled, and the family and I were ready to plant roots in one place.

My follow-on assignment after leaving the 65th Squadron was to be Director of Plans in the Tactical Fighter Weapons Center (TFWC). The commander was my boss and was a two-star major general. It was not a bad job as staff officers' jobs go but was not a flying position.

I had received an invitation from the Daedalian Flight at McChord AFB, Tacoma, Washington. Daedalians had to be pilots who were nominated to join the select organization. Most of them at McChord AFB had multi-engine experience but wanted a briefing on the history and mission of the Aggressors since it was the Air Force equivalent to the Navy Top Gun Squadron. I accepted and looked forward to flying there, spending the night after my presentation, and flying back to Nellis in the morning.

I visited the wing commander (a brigadier general) for approval to take an airplane for the trip. He did not want to approve it because I was changing jobs. I explained that I had accepted the invitation, and it would be good publicity for Nellis AFB. Plus, flying my own F-5E was probably cheaper and much more convenient. I convinced him in my favor.

The day of my speech, I flew from Las Vegas to Tacoma, got my room on base, got dressed, and joined the Daedalians for dinner and my presentation. I did my part and answered several questions. The audience was enlightened on what and how we were training pilots of all services and even foreign military pilots in air-to-air engagements so they would be better prepared for aerial combat than we were going into the Vietnam War. It was fun to be with fellow aviators especially since I was also a Daedalian. I was happy for the opportunity.

The next morning, I flew back to Nellis AFB as planned. I entered the traffic pattern and landed on runway 03 left, basically south to north. My last landing in the F-5E was good, and I knew that was the end of my military flying career.

However, after all my experience in training, instructing, in combat, in emergencies, etc., there had to be one more thing to help remember this final flight. As I rolled out and turned off the runway, I retarded the throttles to idle to taxi to my parking spot. In doing so, the right engine flamed out. Of course, for me, nothing could be routine. I was convinced it was a problem with the throttle stop slipping, so I just ignored the problem and taxied my airplane to parking. I wrote up the malfunction, told the crew chief about it, walked away, and hung up my parachute and helmet thinking, *My fighter experience began with a fire light on my first fighter flight and ended with an engine flameout on my last fighter flight. Why do I find myself in these situations?*

Northrop F-5E Aggressor, last flight taxiing in

CHAPTER 15

★

Airshows

Worldwide air shows draw large crowds of spectators. It is exciting to share the aircraft noise, performances, beauty, and daredevil stunts displayed by all kinds of airplanes at air shows. As a family of five pilots, we are very big air show fans. It is also a privilege that each of us has participated, in various ways, to make air shows successful and rewarding to the attending crowds. The following are narratives of five separate air shows in which I had the privilege to be a featured flying participant.

LANGLEY AFB, HAMPTON, VIRGINIA—MAY 1964

I was a first lieutenant serving as training officer and standardization/evaluation instructor and check pilot at HQ TAC. My duties included monitoring, scheduling, and flying with almost 180 jet pilots in the HQ. Of course, I had help from three other pilots who were senior to me.

Langley AFB was part of a community hosting Air Force, Army, and Navy organizations. Langley hosted an Armed Forces Day celebration with displays and an air show. It drew large crowds, and 1964 was no exception with approximately forty-seven thousand spectators. The organizers of the event could not schedule the AF Thunderbirds air show team even though they were part of TAC. There were two pilots, the Patillo brothers, in staff jobs at our headquarters who were former Thunderbirds with plenty of air show experience. They were asked to fly a demonstration at the scheduled air show, but both declined. They admitted they were not currently proficient enough in our T-33 jets to safely fly an air show demonstration. None of the other staff pilots were considered for the same reason.

When I heard of the dilemma, I told my boss that I could fly a credible acrobatic demonstration in the air show. I devised a series of acrobatic maneuvers that were approved by the powers-at-be and was given the assignment to prepare for the air show. I was given an airplane in which to practice and scheduled three or four practice shows.

My practice sessions were over the outer banks of Virginia across the Chesapeake Bay. It was a short flight and allowed plenty of time to organize and rehearse my proposed air show. The T-33 was normally configured with two fuel tanks mounted on the wingtips. I asked the crew chief to remove the empty tanks. Without them, I could accelerate faster, maintain higher airspeeds, fly a couple of maneuvers that were not possible with tanks, and still have enough fuel for my show.

The repertoire went like this: several fast aileron rolls the length of the runway, four point roll, eight point roll, loop, Cuban eight, and a slow speed rudder roll with the landing gear extended. The final maneuver was a double Immelmann. I had never seen anyone perform this maneuver before, and I had never seen a slow speed rudder roll with the landing gear down performed before, so I practiced them to make sure they were safe. I made the approaches at five hundred feet from the crowd and only two hundred feet above the ground. Coming into land, I performed a three-quarter roll in the opposite direction of the landing pattern and pulled up to a normal downwind with a routine landing.

My air demonstration was the highlight of the show because I was the only jet-performing acrobatics and making noise. Before I got in the airplane to taxi for takeoff, I pulled our three little boys around the displays in our wagon in my flying suit. My good friend Bob Coates took care of the boys while I was occupied flying because my wife was in Richmond, Virginia, on a church assignment and did not see the show nor could she tend our sons while I was performing.

After I landed, parked the T-33, hung up my helmet and parachute, I just blended back into the crowd with my three little boys riding in the wagon. It was a fun day.

ABBOTSFORD, BRITISH COLUMBIA, CANADA—SUMMER 1976

This air show is the third largest in the world only behind Farnborough, England, and Paris, France. In 1976, I was flying with a Canadian fighter squadron at Cold Lake, Alberta, Canada, when they received an invitation to participate for three days in Abbotsford. It was a unique privilege because there were aircraft from as far away as Europe. There were three or four pilots who immediately volunteered to participate. The problem was no one felt qualified nor had the desire to lead a flight of four CF-5s. At the time, I was the operations officer (second-in-command of the squadron) and mentioned I had a lot of experience leading flights in combat, etc. and would be happy to lead the flight if they wanted me to do so. They jumped right on that suggestion, and we began planning our air show.

We practiced a few times at our home base. The wingmen did an excellent job flying their formation positions. The day before our first performance, we left Cold Lake and flew to Comox Canadian Forces Base, a few miles north of Abbortsford, British Columbia. I reviewed with the team our plan, events of the next day, and several relevant points that were important to our timing and communication with the air show coordinator.

Obviously, we could not mimic the Canadian Snowbirds or the US Thunderbirds with formation acrobatics. Our participation would be to represent a first-line Canadian fighter squadron that stood ready to defend their country or to support allies in any world location. Our show, with camouflaged fighters, would demonstrate assets available on a moment's notice to defend against enemies who might attempt to take away other's freedoms.

We made several passes in different close formations. First was the standard formation with two wingmen on one side and one wingman on the opposite side. Next was a diamond with one wingman on each side and one behind and a little below the leader (in the slot) in close formation with all four aircraft. Echelon formation was demonstrated with three aircrafts closely lined on the same side. The last pass was in trail with all four aircrafts' nose to tail behind the aircraft in front. Since this was the final pass, we selected full afterburners, pulled up in a sixty degree climb, and rolled several times. Each wingman followed my example, and we departed the show.

Abbotsford Airshow,
Alston leading

Abbotsford Airshow,
diamond formation

We gave a good show with the maneuvers flown. The narrator introduced each member of the team, and our mission in the Canadian Air Force. I was very happy with the performance and the professional flying of my wingmen. The only thing that gave me pause was when we returned home.

At church, the next Sunday, a member, who was at the air show, approached me with his accolades of our participation at Abbotsford. It made me proud until he said, "How come a United States Air Force pilot led a Canadian demonstration team in Canadian airplanes at a Canadian air show?" I swallowed hard and only said, "Because there was no one in the squadron who was qualified or who wanted to be the leader." We parted friends, and fortunately, it was never mentioned again on future Sundays.

WENDOVER, UTAH—AUGUST 12, 1990

Wendover airport is on Interstate 80 in a remote area on the Utah west desert at the border with Nevada. Historically, it was the site for training the Enola Gay B-29 bomber that dropped the atomic bomb on Hiroshima, Japan, ending World War II. It is an active airport and is used by many students training flights because it is never busy, has runway lights at night, and an instrument approach. It is ideal for an air show because of flat terrain.

A show was scheduled for a weekend in hopes of drawing a good crowd. People drove, several flew in, and there were many privately owned airplanes. The organizers tried to get the Air Force Thunderbirds, but they were unable to work it into their schedule. For display, there were two T-33 jet trainers. One painted white with red tip tanks and the other was painted like a Navy Blue Angel (navy acrobatic air show team). Additionally, there was a Learjet, British Folland Gnat (a supersonic trainer), and a World War II P-51 fighter.

The first event of the show was an air race. I had never flown in an air race, and I do not think anyone else had either. There were three pylons set in a triangle. The racers flew as low as they dared which was about one hundred feet maximum. There were only three participants: a twin-engine Lear business jet, the British Gnat, and the red and white T-33 that I flew since I had retired from the AF.

The start began fine with all three of us lined abreast at the starting point. After the start, it was every man for himself to go as fast as possible, round the pylons as close as possible, and not hit another airplane. The race was basically between the Gnat and the T-33. The Learjet did the best he could until they "over temped" the engines with the high-power settings and had to drop out of the race.

I was not nervous flying close to the ground because I had done a lot of low-level flying in my air force career but trying not to hit the Gnat around the pylons was nerve-racking. The two of us stayed close throughout all circuits around the pylons and were together on the final sprint to the finish. I got all I could out of the T-bird, but the smaller and sleeker Gnat pulled away and beat me by less than five-hundred feet.

With the race over, the Lear and Gnat landed, and I stayed airborne to give my practiced acrobatic air show of several different rolls, loop, Cuban eight, Immelmann, etc. I had performed a practice show and discussed regulations with a Federal Aviation Agency (FAA) representative, so I was certified legal to perform in civilian air shows.

It gave me a good feeling as I taxied to parking with the crowd cheering and waving. I guess they liked the show. However, I was very satisfied to share the day with my wife, Patsy, and our son, Brad, who is also a pilot.

WEST JORDAN, UTAH—JUNE 1–3 1990

This was a really fun show in which to participate. The location was in Salt Lake Valley, where we lived, so it was a short drive for our friends and neighbors. It was also the airport where we hangered our own airplane. We knew all the people associated with the airport and who would be working the shows and displays. In addition to my flying the featured acrobatic demonstration in the T-33 jet, three of our sons contributed. Our oldest son, Doug, was stationed overseas at the time so he was absent. Brad was the air boss and controlled all flying operations. Russ brought an air force trainer to be displayed. Rod was my crew chief and operated the ground equipment for engine starts and controlled all ground procedures. A local TV channel covered the show, and the reporter just happened to be a cousin of our daughter-in-law. She interviewed us, put it on the six and ten o'clock news, and gave us a copy of the tape.

TV interview at West Jordan Airshow

The airspace around the airport was restricted from other airplanes so we could operate unrestricted. However, our airspace only went to five thousand feet above the ground because of airline traffic on approach to Salt Lake International Airport. The ceiling barely gave me enough room to fly a loop and Cuban eight. Everything else was close to the ground in front of the crowd.

There were several other airplanes that performed in the show, but I was the final act. I performed my usual acrobatic maneuvers and kept the airplane close to the airport, so the crowd never lost sight of me even between acrobatic events. I reversed courses from right to left and vice versa using a climbing turn within airport property then diving to gain airspeed for the next event. I heard later that the crowd loved keeping me in sight the entire show.

The show director wanted to demonstrate strafing ground targets. My T-33 did not have guns, so I simulated strafing passes while they detonated pyrotechnics on the ground. It looked and sounded real to the spectators, and I logged a little more flying time.

It was a fun three days. I saw many friends and made more friends who came to the airplane after my show. It was still fun to fly a jet after retiring from the air force, specially to show off precision acrobatics. I am a lucky man.

HILL AIR FORCE BASE, UTAH—JUNE 27, 1992

Hill is a large air force base in my home state and was only about thirty-five miles north of our home. The show was a two-day event drawing huge crowds. It is held every other year, and the Thunderbirds always come to participate in this event. There are many aircraft on display including some you can enter and see inside, including the cockpit. There are several flying acts that last through the day leading to the final act performed by the Thunderbirds at the end of the day.

The red and white T-33 that I had been flying was included in the show to be on display and to fly. I was the only pilot flying that airplane that was qualified and certified by the FAA for such an event. I was all in. Our son, Brad, served as my crew chief, and we delivered the T-33 to our spot at Hill AFB on a Friday.

Since both of us love air shows, we arrived at Hill AFB before the general public was allowed to storm the entrance gates. We were able to visit the displays and still be at our airplane to greet spectators and answer their questions.

My flying portion of the show was in the afternoon just before the Thunderbirds took off for the final act. Brad got me started, and I took off and performed my usual exciting repertoire of acrobatic maneuvers. After landing, I had friends come to the airplane to shake my hand and look over the airplane. They were thrilled when I allowed them to sit in the cockpit. I hoped my show inspired the Thunderbird pilots to try to outdo me with their demonstration…just kidding. It was fun for all of us including the thousands of spectators.

CHAPTER 16

★

Ferry Flights

This is a collection of selected military and civilian flights of similar purpose. Ferry flights are simply taking an airplane from one place and delivering it to another. Reasons for ferry flights include maintenance at a specific location that is not available at the home base, transfer of ownership from one entity to another, or delivery to the boneyard where military airplanes are retired from their flying lives. During ferry flights, pilots can enjoy navigational proficiency, see new landscapes, record flight time in the logbook, and have a lot of fun.

F-86L

My first opportunity was to ferry an F-86L from Salt Lake City, Utah, to Sacramento, California. The purpose was to deliver the aircraft to McClellan AFB—the depot where major overhaul could be accomplished and then return the airplane as good as new. I had never landed at McClellan before, so I was able to see a new airfield. There was a little paperwork in the receiving office to turn over the airplane and maintenance forms. Mission accomplished, I flew home via Western Airlines.

In 1962, our ANG squadron was converting from all-weather interceptors to multi-engine cargo aircraft. As a result, we were taking our F-86Ls to the boneyard (the 309th Aerospace Maintenance and

Regeneration Group in Tucson, Arizona). I was one of four pilots selected to deliver airplanes one summer day. The boneyard is part of Davis-Monthan AFB. The flight was enjoyable flying formation and landing at a base that I had not visited previously. After landing, we taxied behind a "Follow Me" truck who led the way. We even had to wait at a red light until it turned green to cross the highway before entering the area where acres of all types of airplanes were stored. It was almost breathtaking to see. Since the airplanes would never fly again, each of us stole the small Batori computer that was under the right canopy sill. It was my only souvenir, and I still have it. The flight back to Salt Lake City was not as enjoyable because it was in a two-engine C-47 "goony bird." It was hot, cruised at a low altitude, and cruised at less than 200 knots (230 mph). What made it worse was a couple of fighter pilot buddies got airsick; I was not one of them. We missed flying in jet fighters.

T-33

While stationed at Langley AFB, Virginia, I had two opportunities to ferry airplanes. The first began when I received a telephone call from my good friend, Major Bob Coates, who worked in TAC HQ. He had volunteered to fly a T-33 from Springfield, Ohio, to Montevideo, Uruguay, needed a second pilot, and asked if I would like to go with him. I think I answered yes before he finished his question. Our plan was to alternate seats in the T-33 jet trainer every flight so we could take turns being pilot-in-command.

We traveled by commercial airline from Newport News, Virginia, to Ohio and took possession of the T-33. Our first flight was in the afternoon to Randolph AFB, San Antonio, Texas, where we spent the night. In the morning, we flew to Mexico City for fuel. The airport elevation is 7, 343 feet, quite a difference from our base at sea level. From there, we flew to Nicaragua for fuel and to spend the night. Just the week before we were there, the airport had been shelled by enemy guerillas. The runway was not damaged, but we could see craters in the grassy infield. We were safe having dinner and spending the night, but I was happy when we left the next morning.

Day three took us to Panama City, Panama. Before we landed, we toured the Panama Canal from the air. It was fun to fly from the Atlantic Ocean—a short distance to the Pacific Ocean in just a few seconds. We spent the night, and Bob had a friend, who was stationed there, showed us around the city before we had dinner and settled in for the night.

Day four, with me as pilot-in-command, got us to South America with a planned refueling stop at Guayaquil, Ecuador. The international airport is near the city and is close to the coast of the Pacific Ocean. However, our flight plan was to land at the Ecuadorian Air Force base which was east of the city in the jungle. We could not find the airfield. There was no navigational aid to help. We plotted a vector from the international airport beacon to the base location shown on our map and flew it with no success. We agreed to fly an ever-enlarging square over the jungle to see if we could search and find the runway before running out of fuel. After three or four circuits, we located the runway, received landing clearance, and safely concluded this leg of the trip. While we were being refueled, the officer who met and welcomed us took us to their club for lunch. After the trouble we had finding the runway, the lunch and friendly reception were a welcomed break. We were airborne an hour later.

Our next stop was Lima, Peru. Flying down the west coast of South America was beautiful. We saw the Pacific Ocean off the right wing and the Andes Mountains off the left. Since most places had no meteorological service, we talked with airliners to get and give weather observations of our routes to and from landing airports. We ate a nice café supper and spent the night in a hotel.

Day five included a refueling stop in Antofagasta, Chile. It was in the middle of what looked like a vast desert and was easy to find after flying a thousand miles from Lima. Just for practice, we flew a simulated flameout approach to landing. With replenished tanks full of jet fuel, we were off again for Santiago, Chile, where we spent the night.

We only had one more day of flying before delivering the airplane to the Uruguayan Air Force. The last leg was interesting because we took off near the Pacific Ocean, climbed over the high

Andes Mountains, and landed on the east coast of South America next to the Atlantic Ocean. We spent the rest of the day and night in Montevideo, Uruguay, and visited the beach the next day in short sleeves because it was summer in that hemisphere. Our return was uneventful after we boarded a Boeing 747 airliner, took off from Montevideo, and flew the short distance to Buenos Aires, Argentina, for more passengers. It was a nonstop ten-hour flight to New York City. The end of the adventure was sitting on plush seats instead of a parachute and letting other pilots fly us back to Newport News, Virginia, and home. It was a great trip with many new experiences even without understanding Spanish.

T-33

The next ferry flight only took three days. It also originated from Langley AFB with a commercial flight to Oakland California to get the airplane. After taking care of the paperwork, I took off with another pilot, and we flew from the sunny climate of the west coast to landing in a snowstorm at Malmstrom AFB, Great Falls, Montana, where we spent the night.

The weather was a little better in the morning, and it was my copilot's turn to fly from Montana to Whitehorse, Yukon Territory, Canada. Whitehorse is a historic mining town and claims to have more bars on the main street than any place in the world. We did not visit any of the bars but ate lunch and wandered the streets to see the local sites. There is a large river on the edge of town where we saw old-style river barges that transported supplies and people to the mining camps. It really is a fascinating town.

We finally took off and headed north for Alaska. It was a clear day, and from approximately 180 miles away, we could see Denali (formerly Mount McKinley, renamed in 2015). Denali is the highest mountain in North America and the third highest mountain in the world behind Mount Everest and Aconcagua. I asked the other pilot to check the map for Denali's elevation. It showed the peak was 20, 310 feet above sea level. I made sure I had a current and accurate altimeter setting and informed my back seat pilot that I was going to level our altitude at twenty-one thousand feet and go right over the summit of the mountain. The closer we got, the more my anxiety grew. I was not convinced that 690 feet was enough. I was prepared to pull back on the control stick just in case. I flew right over the summit and followed with two or three circles around the mountain just below the summit. It was a magnificent sight flying that close and was certainly more impressive than when I viewed it from the ground two hundred miles away years later.

After our fun, I landed at Elmendorf AFB, Anchorage, Alaska, and handed over the T-33. We walked around town viewing the recent damage from a large earthquake, had a nice fish dinner, and spent the night. In the morning, we caught a commercial flight and returned to our homes in Virginia. I love flying to new places.

F-104C

During my first combat tour at Da Nang AB, South Vietnam, our maintenance inspections were accomplished at Kung Kuan AB, Taichung, Taiwan. Each of us was given the opportunity to deliver an airplane and spend a few days away from combat on rest and rec-reation (R & R). We did not have air to air refueling support, so it required two flights. My turn came after my twenty-fifth mission when I joined Jack Gale, who was my flight commander, and John Olson, another member of our flight. Jack led us across the South China Sea (about seven hundred miles) to Clark AFB, Manila, Philippines. After refueling the airplanes, we took off again and flew north to Taiwan. We spent twelve days in Taichung; it was a needed rest. I got to fly an FCF flight, and John and I took a train to Taipei—the capital of the country on the north end of the island. After four days, we returned, on the train, in the middle of a typhoon. Our hotel room had no power, but we were out of the rain and wind. Jack left before the typhoon and flew an F-104 back to Da Nang. John and I were left to return to Da Nang the next day with the other two airplanes.

John led us to the Philippines for our refueling stop, and I led the flight to Da Nang with John in formation on my left wing. After taking off, my navigation equipment failed, so I called John to take the lead, but his radio transmitter had failed and refused to lead. We entered solid clouds after takeoff and were in them all the way to thirty-five thousand feet. The F-104 has very short and thin wings, and there were times I could not see John. I mentioned that if he could not maintain visual formation on the wing to get underneath me where he had the larger fuselage to keep in sight. He did it several times.

I held a preplanned heading across the sea but was concerned about crosswind blowing us off our track. About one hundred miles from Da Nang, I began to descend to see if the weather was better. At four thousand feet, we were still in the clouds. The Da Nang approach control identified us on their radar, and they relayed a weather report for Da Nang that was optimistic. I descended to two thousand feet and still could not see anything but rain and white caps on the sea below.

It got close to my computed flight time, and we still could not see anything but clouds. I had a bad feeling that I was lost. Fortunately, we passed a small island that I recognized as Monkey Mountain where the radar antenna was located. I breathed a sigh of relief, flew another sixty seconds, and made a gentle left turn where we broke out of the clouds into clear weather. We visually acquired the base, and all the "butterflies" left my stomach. We landed, parked, and looked around the area from the ground. The only good weather was a "cylinder" clear of clouds and rain about eight miles in diameter right over Da Nang.

My navigation might have been blind luck, but I think I had heavenly help navigating with me. John and I were glad to be safely on the ground.

F-104G

We had a large fleet of F-104Gs at Luke AFB, Arizona, and occasionally, airplanes had to be flown to the Lockheed plant at Palmdale, California, for major maintenance that could not be performed by the air force. There was usually no advanced notice to find a pilot to make the flight. It was difficult because word usually came about the time everyone was going home, especially on a Friday when beer call was beckoning. Orders had to be obtained, flight plans filed, and it was just a big hassle.

My close friend and fellow F-104 instructor, Jerry Friedman, and I discussed the issue and arrived at a solution to present to the director of operations (DO). Together, we visited the DO, who was a full colonel, and proposed the two of us be placed on permanent orders to be designated pilots to ferry the airplanes. We guaranteed that one or both of us would make ourselves available at a moment's notice to accomplish ferry flights to and from Palmdale. He agreed it would solve the problem, would eliminate one of his headaches, and was happy to make it happen. From that time, during our assignments at Luke AFB, Jerry and I were the only pilots who accomplished these flights. Many times, we had two fighters or a two-seat trainer to move so both of us could go together.

Palmdale was only about thirty minutes away from Luke, so we usually filed a flight plan to add a little more flying time. We flew to the Mexican border then north over Los Angeles where we had fun doing aileron rolls or rolling around each other. After our fun, we descended and landed at the Palmdale airport. If we had airplanes to return to Luke, we took them back home, and if it was a one-way trip, we flew commercial airline flights to or from where the airplanes were located. It was fun; we logged more flying time, did not have to deal with students, and made everyone else happy that we took on the responsibility and relieved them of last-minute panics.

OTHERS

I could also include T-33 ferry flights, as a civilian, from Grand Junction, Colorado, to Salt Lake City, Utah; Salt Lake City, Utah to Boise, Idaho; Wendover, Utah, to Pocatello, Idaho; Mohave, California, to Salt Lake City. Or how about ferry flights in a Cessna 172 from Bountiful, Utah, to Boise, Idaho, a Cessna 206 from Idaho Falls, Idaho to Salt Lake City, Utah, or a Cessna 210 from Salt Lake City to Cedar City, Utah. You get the idea, so I will not bore you with details but which were a lot of fun at the time. You would have enjoyed flying in the other seat on any of those trips.

CHAPTER 17

★

General Aviation

Yes, fellow pilots, there is life after the air force. Probably, the most attractive industry is the commercial airline business. It is reasonable to assume that the attraction is to continue flying airplanes, and secondarily, with seniority, you might make more money than the government paid for your twenty or more years. However, there are a lot of other flying experiences in the civilian world that are just as fulfilling and safer than the military because no enemy shoots at you. Try it; you will like it. The following are just a few examples of memorable flights post air force.

CAPSULE RECOVERY TEST

I don't know all the details about this, but basically, NASA had scheduled a small, unmanned capsule to be launched from Wallops Island, Virginia. The recovery system was manufactured by a company in California and was to be tested in Utah where it would be recovered on reentry from the actual test. I was asked to participate in the test, flying a civilian-owned T-33.

My first requirement was to attend and participate in the premission briefing at Hill AFB where each test point was discussed, and requirements were assigned. The capsule was to be carried by a civilian-owned B-57 Canberra that would launch from Boise, Idaho, climb to its maximum altitude, and release the capsule recovery system over the Utah Test Range. My job was to dive with the test item, keep it in sight, and locate it after it landed on the ground.

Martin B-57 Canberra

I had to preposition the T-33 to Boise, Idaho from Salt Lake City, Utah, so it gave me an opportunity to take my wife, Patsy, in the back seat. Brad flew our Cessna T210 to bring his mother back to Salt Lake City. I had to stay the night and fly the mission the next day. I let her fly the jet, perform aileron rolls, and was proud of her being my copilot. She enjoyed the flight and the experience to see what it is like to be a jet pilot.

The B-57 pilot and I discussed every aspect of the flight and how we would fly the mission to the test range in Utah. In my back seat was the company engineer who designed the capsule recovery system. I took off in formation with the B-57, and we flew a continual climb toward the drop area. At approximately forty-one thousand feet, the B-57 stopped climbing because his engines were starting to exceed safe temperatures; we were high enough anyhow.

Reaching the drop point, I received a countdown. On release, I began my circling dive to keep the capsule in sight. At the proper time, the recovery parachute was deployed, and it became easier to keep it in sight and follow to landing on the desert floor. We orbited at low altitude to mark the area so the recovery team could find and retrieve the capsule.

Having done our job, I turned toward Salt Lake City and landed to complete my responsibilities. My passenger was happy, thanked me for the part I played, and paid me generously. I could make a living with flights like that.

AERIAL PHOTOGRAPHY AND MAPPING

I was hired to fly for a survey company which was very active in aerial photography work. We took photos for many reasons such as train and truck incidents, coal pile volume inventories, construction sites, open pit mines, roads, mountains, deserts, industrial plants, and anything else that customers ordered.

I flew a Cessna T206 Stationair (turbocharged) that had the rear seats removed and an eighteen-inch hole cut in their place with a large camera mounted over the hole. I flew the airplane and carried a photographer to operate the camera.

Cessna T206 Stationair

Our jobs were only flown on good weather days because shadows were unacceptable and clear sunny skies provided the best contrast. Most of our business was in Utah, Idaho, and Wyoming, but we also flew jobs in Montana, Nevada, Arizona, California, Colorado,

183

Oregon, and, believe it or not, Illinois, West Virginia, Georgia, and Texas.

Depending on the requirements, we flew as low as five hundred feet above the ground to twenty-five thousand feet above sea level. Many times, we had to make stops at small or remote airports to refuel.

The actual lines we photographed in my first few years were solely made visually by choosing a distant mountain or other easily discernable point and flying a perfect altitude to maintain the desired scale. The wings had to be level so the photos were accurate on the required line. It was easier and much more efficient when we installed a global positioning system (GPS). Even with a crosswind, staying on a line was easy after getting GPS; I never had to repeat a line.

When I was not flying for my employer, I occasionally filled in for two other companies as their backup pilot. One company also used a Cessna T206, and the other company used a Cessna T210. I liked it because our family airplane was that model. It was faster and had retractable landing gear that the 206 did not have. It was a great part-time job. I made good money and accumulated a lot of flying time.

CESSNA T206 EMERGENCY

I have written about several malfunctions or emergencies I experienced while flying military aircraft. Well, the same can occur in general aviation flying. This was a routine photo job that we had done before and was repeated four or five times a year. On this occasion, we took off from Salt Lake City to fly north to an open pit mine just east of Dillon, Montana.

I thought it was a good day to stay low and enjoy seeing farms, towns, and animals on the way. I leveled at eight thousand feet above sea level, and my photographer and I talked about various sites as we passed them. Our course took us close to Idaho Falls, Idaho. They have a very nice airport at an elevation of 4,700 feet. We had landed there on previous occasions.

We passed the city, and I had a prompting to climb another two thousand feet. We did not need the extra altitude to clear the hills ahead, but it was such a clear mental suggestion that I could not ignore it. I leveled the airplane at ten thousand feet and felt comfortable with the change.

We had only gone thirty or forty miles north of Idaho Falls when there was a loud bang from the engine resulting in significant vibrations. My photographer looked at me and asked, "What was that?" My answer was "I don't know." That was the truth because it was something new to me, but I knew it was potentially serious.

Immediately, I turned around toward Idaho Falls and looked below us for fields or roads that might be possible emergency landing sites. Simultaneously, I reduced the throttle to idle hoping we could make it to the Idaho Falls airport. The low power reduced the vibrations but did not eliminate them.

I called the Idaho Falls tower, declared an emergency, gave our location and intention. They responded normally with the active runway instructions. Unfortunately, they were landing and taking off on runway 35 which is to the north. I reported that we were losing altitude, had no engine power, and requested a straight-in approach to runway 17. If they had any traffic at the time, they held them away from the runway and cleared me as I requested.

We landed safely with little margin to spare. Since we were safely on the ground and the engine was still running, I taxied to the ramp in front of the tower and requested a mechanic to meet us. We removed the left side cowling to look at the engine. The mechanic found the last of the oil dripping out of a cylinder that had a catastrophic failure and split off a piece of metal housing a valve.

We could not have made the airport without the additional two thousand feet of altitude that I was prompted to gain. Our alternative was to land in a farmer's field probably resulting in more damage. The cylinder was replaced, and I returned a couple of weeks later, test flew the airplane, and returned it to Salt Lake City. We failed to photograph the mine east of Dillon, Montana. Sorry folks, please give us another opportunity.

CESSNA T210 FIRST FLIGHT

Our sons and I bought a 1969 Cessna T210 Centurion. It had not flown for almost a year because it was too complicated of an airplane for the owner. We had our local aircraft mechanic check everything he could and sign off an annual inspection to comply with FAA requirements. None of us had flown anything but a Cessna 172. The differences were many. The Centurion had six cylinders that developed 285 turbocharged horsepower, was capable of cruising at two hundred mph, carried ninety gallons of fuel, had retractable landing gear, six seats, and was capable of climbing to twenty-five thousand feet. A Cessna 172 Skyhawk originally had a 145-horsepower engine, carried 56 gallons of fuel, held four people (including the pilot), could barely climb to 13,500 feet, and maximum speed was 140 mph. You get the idea if you are not already familiar with the two airplanes.

Cessna T210J Centurion

When we were ready to test fly it, my wife, Patsy, and two sons Douglas and Bradley wanted to go on the test flight. I was in the left pilot seat and Douglas, who had many hours in a Cessna 172, sat in the right pilot seat with the others strapped in behind us. None of us had flown an aircraft like this, but we had read the manual. We taxied to the runway, checked the engine and controls, then took off. Doug and I each flew the new airplane just to get the feel of it. Everything went well, and we were happy with our purchase.

We turned toward the airport and moved the landing gear lever to the down position. Guess what? You guessed it. The landing gear did not lock in the down position. That was a hydraulic problem to be fixed when we got on the ground. In the meantime, Brad consoled his mother who was nervous about the problem and anticipated a gear-up landing.

However, following the emergency procedure, Doug used the emergency hand pump and was able to extend the landing gear to full down and locked positions. We made our first landing and returned the airplane to the mechanic to work on the landing gear system. All is well that ends well, and the airplane never repeated the problem in the twenty-five years we owned it.

Postscript: Besides me, all four of our sons flew the airplane. Patsy and I used it to visit our boys and their families when they lived out of state; Doug and Russ flew their share, and Brad began his flying as a glider pilot and added his private pilot license evaluation in the T210 then took it to Mexico. Rod trained and successfully passed his FAA private pilot license evaluation flight in the T210 as well. That is impressive because most new pilots do not fly a complex aircraft like that for their check flight. However, Rod is a quick study, as are each of our sons, because now he is a corporate pilot flying a Gulfstream 550 all over the world.

LAST CIVILIAN FLIGHT

I decided to stop flying. Our sons were all back in Utah; we sold our T210 as fuel cost became expensive, and I had enjoyed many years as a pilot. The previous year, I mentioned to Patsy that I was going to quit flying. She encouraged me to keep my physical exam current, to receive an annual flight check, and fly another year. Like a dutiful husband, I complied with her suggestions.

One morning about a year later, I told Patsy I was going to the airport and fly my last flight as a rated pilot. She jumped all over that and replied she was going with me. I told her I was going to fly alone for the last time. She did not want to fly with me but wanted to take photographs of the occasion.

At the airport, Patsy took pictures of our son Russell's Cessna 172, previously owned by his brother Doug. I gave Patsy our hand-held radio tuned to the airport frequency so she could listen to my radio calls on takeoff and landing. I told her I was going to play for a while, and on my return, I would end the flight with my first perfect landing.

Last flight taxi for takeoff

Everything went as planned. I was the only airplane in the traffic pattern. I made the standard position reports on the radio so Patsy would know I was coming back. My first traffic pattern was good, and I made a good landing, but I felt the wheels touch the runway, not good enough. So I added power and took off again. The second pattern was good, and I concentrated on the final approach. This time I touched down without feeling the tires meet the runway surface. I had met my desired landing standard, so I returned the airplane to its hanger and stepped away.

Fifty-five years of flying was over.

Last flight after fifty-five years of flying

EPILOGUE

★

My air force career began on February 7, 1954, when I was sworn in with the beginning rank of airman basic. I was assigned to the 130th Aircraft and Warning Squadron in the Utah Air National Guard. My specialty was radio repairman. We had all-day training the first Saturday and Sunday of every month and fifteen days of full-time training in the summer. I learned to march, salute, attend lectures about radios, learned Morse code, and mingled with other airmen. There were no women in the squadron at that time.

My air force flying career began in jet fighters and ended in jet fighters. Of course, there were occasional diversions in nonflying jobs, but the air force specialty code remained a fighter pilot, and I always returned to my love of flying.

I had the privilege of flying twenty-seven different military airplanes during my twenty-four years as an air force pilot. My official flight records a total of 5,385.3 flying hours in the following distribution: student, 245.1; pilot-in-command, 2,598.7; instructor pilot, 2,409.4; and copilot, 132.1. Included in the total are 282.4 combat hours. I had 136 combat missions topped off with the honor of being the first pilot in the US Air Force to be credited with 100 combat missions over North Vietnam in the F-104 Starfighter.

100th mission airplane paperwork   100th mission complete!

I progressed from pilot to senior pilot to command pilot in minimum times and always maintained an instrument rating. I was upgraded to flight leader in every aircraft including leading combat flights after my fifth mission. Fifteen years after receiving my original pilot wings, I received an additional rating as a qualified parachutist which added another silver badge to my uniform.

As an Air Force officer, we are responsible for many other duties in addition to flying airplanes. I was the "snack bar officer" which is reserved for the lowest-ranking pilot in a fighter squadron. I taught air combat maneuvering and weapons delivery to F-104 pilots at Luke AFB Fighter University. I was a controller in a wing command post and still flew as an instructor.

During my career, additional duties included functional check pilot (maintenance test pilot), ferry pilot, Air Officer Commanding of Cadet Squadron 27 at the USAF Academy, executive officer for two commandants of cadets at the academy. I was a standardization evaluation flight examiner, assistant flight commander, flight commander, operations officer, and squadron commander. I have been a member of accident investigations—special assistant with responsibility to write and conduct practice emergency base exercises. I conducted base inspections for compliance of regulations and approved procedures. I served as Assistant Director of Plans at the AF Fighter Weapons Center and later the Director of Plans. I wrote annual officer evaluations for my own people and for my bosses. I gave formal briefings to foreign officers and to high-ranking officers including the Air Force Chief of Staff, chairman of the Joint Chiefs of Staff (four-star generals), and many other high-ranking officers of other services and various major commanders from all around the world. I briefed the National Security Advisor and the Secretary of Defense as well as officers who had been selected for their first star as a brigadier general.

Regardless of the level of duties, or with whom I worked or briefed, I learned valuable lessons that made me a better officer. There were traits I inculcated in my own personality, and there were traits I saw that I quickly discarded and refused to follow their example, regardless of rank or responsibility.

I cannot close without acknowledging the value, fun, friends, and opportunities, doing what I loved, and, most of all, the support of my family. My father was a private during World War I. I have cousins who were pilots in World War II. My sisters' husbands served in Korea (army), in Vietnam (air force), and stateside (army). Two of our sons flew combat in the Iraqi war. Through it all, my wife Patsy kept the home fires burning for us all. She was the perfect wife for me and my career, tolerated the worry of her husband and four sons (who are all pilots) flying at the same time in various situations. She "slipped the surly bonds of earth" herself as she passed away on March 28, 2020, of acute leukemia. Her support, tolerance, advice, and unending love beats all the accolades and medals I have received from my air force career. I served a month short of twenty-eight happy years in the AF, but the sixty-three and a half years married to Patsy is the icing on the cake. *I am blessed that I found myself in that situation.*

Patsy, a fighter pilot's wife

APPENDIX A

★

Aircraft

This is a list of every make or model of aircraft, of any type, in which I have flown, a total of forty-four types.

Hot-air balloon	A fun experience, Park City, Utah, a great gift from Patsy
Schweizer SGS 2-33	Glider, did a loop at AF Academy, two hours flight with Bradley in Utah
Cessna 140	I got my first flight in an airplane
Cessna 172 Skyhawk	Received my first biannual flight check and instrument qualification as a civilian
PT17 Stearman	Open cockpit relic, actual stick time and acrobatics
Cessna 182 Skylane	Salt Lake City to Rock Springs, Wyoming, to pick up a passenger
Cessna T206 Stationaire	Aerial photography jobs
Cessna T210 Centurion	Our family's personal airplane for twenty-five years
Mooney M20	Copilot with Rodney, Salt Lake City to Lubbock, Texas
Beechcraft Bonanza	Copilot from Pocatello, Idaho to Salt Lake City
Beechcraft Baron	Copilot to California and back to Salt Lake City
Beechcraft King Air	Copilot from Dhahran to Jeddah Saudi Arabia
Gulfstream 450	Jet, pilot position with Rodney as copilot, Dallas, Texas, to Provo, Utah
B-25 Mitchell	World War II bomber

AT-6 Texan	Advanced trainer used from 1936 to the early 1950s
T-34 Mentor	Air Force pilot training, first airplane to solo
T-28 Trojan	Air Force pilot training
C-119 Boxcar	Captain and copilot in Air Force Reserve
C-45 Twin Beech	Flew and made landing from Wendover, Utah, to Salt Lake City
C-47 "Goony Bird"	Copilot on test flight
H-21 "Flying Banana"	I had a hard time hovering in one place
F-27 Friendship	Copilot, landed on the Rub al Kali, Saudi Arabia
OV-1 Mohawk	Copilot, Air Force airborne forward air control
T-33 "T-Bird"	First jet, Air Force training and support
CT-33 "T-Bird"	Canadian T-33, engine had more thrust than US models
A-4 Skyhawk	Navy jet fighter/bomber
T-39 Sabreliner	Copilot on a test flight, aileron roll
F-86D Sabre	First fighter, all-weather interceptor
F-86E Sabre	Day fighter
F-86H Sabre	Day fighter
F-86L Sabre	All-weather interceptor
F-89 Scorpion	Idaho ANG interceptor
F-4E Phantom	Air Force first line fighter/bomber
F-100F Super Sabre	At Nellis AFB
CF-101 VooDoo	Canadian all-weather interceptor
CF-5A Freedom Fighter	Canadian fighter/bomber and reconnaissance
CF-5D Freedom Fighter	Canadian two-seat training version of the CF-5A
CF-104D Starfighter	Two-seat Canadian fighter/bomber training version of the CF-104
F-104C Starfighter	Fighter/bomber, 136 combat missions in SE Asia, my favorite
F-104D Starfighter	Two-seat fighter/bomber training version of the F-104C
TF-104G Starfighter	German two-seat fighter training version of the F-104G
F-104G Starfighter	German fighter/bomber
F-5F Tiger Two	AF fighter trainer, Royal Saudi AF and USAF
F-5E Tiger Two	Aggressors, AF equivalent to Navy "Top Gun" aircraft, Last AF flight

APPENDIX B

★

Glossary

A	Attack, a prefix designating aircraft type
AB	Air Base
AC&W	Aircraft Control and Warning
AETE	Aerospace Engineering Testing Establishment, a Canadian organization at Cold Lake, Alberta, Canada
AF	Air Force
AFB	Air Force Base
Agol	The black, round braided head piece that held the gutra in place
ANG	Air National Guard
Angle of Attack	The wings being at too high angle of attack relative to the relative wind
AOC	Air Officer Commanding, a squadron leader at the Air Force Academy
ARAMCO	Arabian American Oil Company
ARTCC	Air Route Traffic Control Center
B	Bomber, a prefix designating aircraft type
B/G	Brigadier general identified with one star
BCT	Basic cadet training
Bogey	Any unidentified aircraft
Break	A hard turn with maximum g force
C	Cargo, a prefix designating aircraft type
CAP	Combat air patrol

CF	Canadian Fighter, a prefix designating aircraft type
CFB	Canadian Forces Base
Col	Colonel
Con	Condensation
DACT	Dissimilar Air Combat Tactics
Deploy	Move from permanent location to a different or temporary location
Doolies	First year cadets at the Air Force Academy
Element	Two fighters in formation
ETP	Equal Time Point
F	Fighter, a prefix designating aircraft type
FAA	Federal Aviation Administration
FAC	Forward Air Controller
FCF	Functional check flight
G	Force of gravity measurement
GCA	Ground controlled approach
GPS	Global Positioning System using an array of fixed satellites in space
Gutra	Head scarf worn by Arabs
H	Helicopter, a prefix designating aircraft type
HQ	Headquarters
HEI	High explosive incendiary (a type of ammunition)
IFR	Instrument flight rules
ILS	Instrument landing system
IP	Initial point
KC	Tanker, a prefix of aircraft type
Knot	Speed measurement (.85 knot = 1 mph)
L	Liaison, a prefix designating aircraft type
Lift	Force created by air flowing over the wings to allow flight
Lt	Lieutenant
Mach	The speed of sound
Meatball	More commonly just called the Ball and is the visual light screen on the left approach end of Navy's aircraft carriers. Actual name is the "Fresnel Lens Optical Landing System."
MiG	Russian Fighter Aircraft made by Mikoyan-Gurevich
MM	Millimeter

MPH	Miles per hour
Ops	Operations
P	Pursuit, a prefix designating aircraft type
POL	Petroleum, oil, lubrication
POW	Prisoner of war
R&R	Rest and Recreation
Redeploy	The opposite of deploy or return to permanent location
RHAW	Radar homing and warning
RPM	Rotations per minute
Recce	Short term for reconnaissance
SAM	Surface-to-air missile
Shamal	Arabic name for a sandstorm
SR	Surveillance, a prefix designating aircraft type
Stall	Result when an airplane does not have enough lift to keep it flying caused by airspeed being too low or from a high angle of attack
T	Trainer, a prefix designating aircraft type
TAC	Tactical Air Command
Tally-ho	Term for visual sighting
TDY	Temporary duty
TFS	Tactical Fighter Squadron
TFW	Tactical Fighter Wing
TFWC	Tactical Fighter Weapons Center
Thobe	Arabic outer garment, a white, one-piece dress like daily attire
Trash Hauler	A fighter pilot's term for any cargo hauling aircraft
U	Utility, a prefix designating aircraft type
UANG	Utah Air National Guard
USAF	United States Air Force
VFR	Visual flight rules

APPENDIX C

★

Photo Credits

Photos taken by the author are noted as copyright © Harold R. Alston.

Photos taken from other sources were not the actual aircraft involved in the story but are for reference only and have not been altered in any way. Specific photo use licenses are cited and abbreviated as shown below.

Creative Commons Zero (CC0)

Creative Commons Zero 1.0 Universal Public Domain Dedication (CC0-UPDD)

Creative Commons Attribution-Share Alike 2.0 Generic (CCA-SA 2.0 Generic)

Creative Commons Attribution-Share Alike 3.0 (CCA-SA 3.0)

Cover Picture	Public domain, USAF photo
Picture 1–8	Copyright © Harold R. Alston
Picture 9–10	Public domain, USAF photo
Picture 11	By Bidgee—Own work, CCA-SA 3.0
Picture 12	Copyright © Harold R. Alston
Picture 13	Public domain, USAF photo
Picture 14	Copyright © Miroslav Hlavko, Shutterstock
Picture 15	By Getty Images
Picture 16–18	Public domain, USAF photo
Picture 19	Unknown

Picture 20–21	Public domain, USAF photo
Picture 22–23	Copyright © Harold R. Alston
Picture 24	By Flyguy71, CCA-SA 2.0 Generic
Picture 25	Public domain, CC0
Picture 26	Unknown
Picture 27–29	Copyright © Harold R. Alston
Picture 30–33	Public domain, USAF photo
Picture 34	Unknown
Picture 35	Copyright © Harold R. Alston
Picture 36–37	Unknown
Picture 38	Public domain, CC0-UPDD
Picture 39–40	Public domain, USAF photo
Picture 41	Public domain, RCAF photo
Picture 42–43	Copyright © Harold R. Alston
Picture 44	Unknown
Picture 45	Copyright © Harold R. Alston
Picture 46	Unknown
Picture 47	Author unknown, CCA-SA 2.0 Generic
Picture 48	Copyright © Harold R. Alston
Picture 49	Unknown (Mig-21), Public domain, USAF photo (F-5E)
Picture 50	Public domain, USAF photo
Picture 51	Public domain, US DoD
Picture 52–54	Copyright © Harold R. Alston
Picture 55	Public domain, USAF photo
Picture 56	Public domain, by Ahunt at English Wikipedia
Picture 57–62	Copyright © Harold R. Alston

ABOUT THE AUTHOR

★

Harold Alston was born in Salt Lake City, Utah. He attended public schools and graduated from the University of Utah with a bachelor's degree in banking and finance. He is an Eagle Scout.

Growing up with three sisters, he and his wife, Patsy, were blessed with four sons. They are grandparents to sixteen and great grandparents to seventeen. He is active in his church and has held lay positions in every place the air force sent him. While having written numerous short articles about family, historical experiences, and original ideas, this is his first book.

After his retirement from the air force, the family returned to Salt Lake City where he currently resides.

CPSIA information can be obtained
at www.ICGtesting.com
Printed in the USA
JSHW050404080222
22696JS00003B/20

9 781638 449256